FINDING GOD IN THE WORLD

FINDING GOD IN THE WORLD

Reflections on a Spiritual Journey

Avery Brooke

1817

Harper & Row, Publishers, San Francisco

New York, Grand Rapids, Philadelphia, St. Louis
London, Singapore, Sydney, Tokyo, Toronto

Grateful acknowledgment is given to the following:
Abingdon Press for permission to quote from *Readings in Christian Thought* by Hugh T. Kerr, p. 33. Doubleday and Company for permission to quote from *India's Walking Saint: The Story of Vinoba Bhave* by Hallam Tennyson, pp. 118–119. Harper & Row, Publishers, Inc., for permission to quote from *Testament of Devotion* by Thomas Kelly, p. 29; *Celtic Prayers* by Avery Brooke, pp. 17–20; *Hymn of the Universe* by Pierre Teilhard de Chardin, p. 36; *The Divine Milieu* by Pierre Teilhard de Chardin, pp. 82–83; *A History of Christian Spirituality, Vol. 2, The Spirituality of the Middle Ages* by Louis Bouyer, Jean Leclercq, and Francois Vandenbroucke, pp. 362–363. Westminster/John Knox Press for permission to quote from *Early Christian Fathers* by Cyril C. Richardson et al., p. 347.

Chapter 16, "Darkness and Light," appeared in a shorter version in *Weavings: A Journal of the Christian Spiritual Life*, Volume II, Number 5, September/October, 1987.

FIRST EDITION

Library of Congress Cataloging-in-Publication Data

Brooke, Avery.
    Finding God in the World: reflections on a spiritual journey / Avery Brooke.
        p.   cm.
    ISBN 0-06-061131-6
    1. Spiritual life.   2. Brooke, Avery.   I. Title.
    BV4501.2.B765   1989
    248.2—dc20   89-45181
                                                                              CIP

89 90 91 92 93 RRD 10 9 8 7 6 5 4 3 2 1

for Dora Chaplin

The primary fact is the confrontation of the human mind with a Something, whose character is only gradually learned, but which is from the first felt as a transcendent presence, "the beyond," even where it is also felt as "the within."

JOHN W. HARVEY

Contents

Preface

The theme of this book centers on how we perceive and respond to God's presence in the world, and I have illustrated it with examples from my own experience. In spite of the personal nature of the writing and the informal style, these chapters are essentially a work of theology. It is my belief that theology is too often set apart as an academic discipline, when its primary place should be in the living of our lives.

All of us have our own theologies, influenced by our religious background, our life experience, and our personality. My own theology, from childhood perceptions of God to the present, has emphasized God's presence within us and within all of the created universe. In formal terms this means the doctrine of Immanence, God's omnipresence in the universe. I have chosen to concentrate on this one aspect of our knowledge of God as I have known it during the course of my life.

Apart from mentioning an author or a book title, I have used a minimum of proper names, as they seemed to distract from ongoing dialogue with or about God. The people, incidents, and circumstances described are, however, as factual as memory will allow, although I have been very selective in what I have recounted, taken a few liberties with time, and occasionally disguised a person or place.

Because I have written for the seeker—whether that seeker knows very little or a great deal about Christianity—I have tried either to use language that may be understood by any reader or to explain theological terms in common language when I introduce them. Theological words are, at best, only human inventions to point toward the Infinite. Sometimes simple words or story point more clearly.

Avery Brooke

Acknowledgments

During the writing of *Finding God in The World*, I received the generous help of many friends. It is impossible to list them all, grateful though I am, but I would like to acknowledge my gratitude to the following people who went out of their way to encourage and advise me:

Chief among them are Shirley Cloyes and Michelle Rapkin who, from my earliest partial drafts, seemed to know instinctively what I was trying to say and believed it should be said. Shirley Cloyes also gave me invaluable editorial help, as did Mary Coelho and Janet Brown. Leonard Krill listened to me *talk* the book for many months and Elizabeth Moynahan listened to me read early drafts and helped to keep me on track. David Kelsey and Francis Tiso gave me their insightful reactions to certain theological issues.

I owe a debt of gratitude to Holy Savior Priory in South Carolina and to St. Deiniol's Library in Wales for providing peaceful places to write. St. Deiniol's also provided a wonderful library, but without the blessed institution of interlibrary loan and research librarian Blanche Parker and her staff at the Darien Library, I would not have been able to finish this book. Finally, I owe more gratitude than I can express to my friend Joan Frank, who typed and retyped the manuscript with both patience and skill and to Janice Johnson, my editor at Harper & Row who ably and wisely guided me through the publishing process.

FINDING GOD IN THE WORLD

1. Within and Beyond

You will find something more in woods than in books. Trees and stones will teach you that which you can never learn from masters.

ST. BERNARD OF CLAIRVAUX

The summer I was ten, my parents bought a house in the country.[1] I put a jackknife on a string around my neck and went exploring. I clambered over stone walls into half-overgrown fields. I trudged through an old New England woodlot as bits of sunlight fell from high above me to dapple the forest floor. I found a great whaleback-shaped rock on a hillside overlooking fields by the river. That summer, and in the years that followed, I grew to know that land and everything that grew there as only a child can know it. I waded in the river, climbed the trees, picked blueberries, cranberries, and grapes. I examined leaves and bark, stones and grasses, and brought them home as treasures. It was to me a virgin world, a Garden of Eden.

A ten year old has a passion for facts and for adventure, and these were supplied in abundance. But as I wandered over the hillside fields and through the woods, I sensed something more, a presence, a power for which I had no explanation. What was it in the sweep of the sky, the giant outcropping of rock, the sassafras leaf in my hand? I did not know, but I felt hushed by awe and a quiet joy. It did not occur to me to connect this "something" with God. My parents were atheists. I can still remember my mother's earnest voice as she told me that she and my father did not believe in God, but that I could believe as I wished. She meant to give me freedom, and in the end it was freedom. But a young child (I must have been seven or eight) presumes that parents must be right. God, therefore, did not exist. I resorted instead to a two-layered handling of the subject. God did not exist, but I could allow myself to suspect the existence of an unexplained "something."

Being free to roam the woods and fields was a new experience for me. Until that spring, the spring of 1933, I had been in the charge of an English nanny. Nanny loved me in her own way, but her main aim in life seemed to be to keep me in spotless frocks and polite before my parents and other nannies.

My mother had what we then called a "nervous breakdown" when I was two. She never fully recovered and slowly retreated from life until she became a recluse. My father was a warm and loving man dedicated to her care. As a young child, I only saw my parents for short visits and I was never taken shopping, out to a restaurant, or on those family expeditions that are part of most children's growing years. My view of the world was very narrow, and I saw it through Nanny's eyes.

Because I had Nanny, there had seemed to be no need to send me to nursery school or kindergarten, so I was six before I started school. I was hopeful but frightened, and fear won. I was constantly saying things that my schoolmates found strange. They teased me, and I cringed. They teased more. They left me out of games and conversations, and if I tried to enter in, they either ignored or scorned me. I lived in fear. I was outside looking in, and I didn't know how to get in. Nanny had taught me that the way to succeed was to behave. But I didn't know how to behave.

My mother and father were, however, the final arbiters in my life. If a question was too big for Nanny, she would say, "Ask your parents."

There was, for instance, the question of Sunday school. Classmates had mentioned it, and I'd asked, "What's Sunday school?" only to be met with exclamations of, "She doesn't even know what Sunday school is!"

One night I asked Nanny, "What's Sunday school? Can I go?"

"You'll have to ask your parents," said Nanny.

The resulting conversation with my mother was the one I referred to earlier in which I discovered that my parents were atheists. The question of going to Sunday school got lost in larger questions about God, but my mother talked with me as if what I thought mattered, and this impressed me. "You can believe as you wish," she said.

We lived across the street from a church,[2] and I remember looking out the window and wondering if I'd have the courage to go and knock on the minister's door and say, "I want to come to Sunday school." I decided I didn't. I know now that my parents would have done the arranging if I'd asked, but I didn't realize that then. I didn't realize many things. What I see and say now about Nanny's influence and the narrowness of my experience was not clear to me then or for many years. In childhood I believed that this was the way the world was. And although I certainly knew how miserable I was in school I did not talk to my parents about this either but eventually someone from school phoned my mother. And so it came about that in the spring I was ten, Nanny was asked to leave and I was told that I was going to a new school in the fall.

It was, therefore, not just discovering the wonders of nature that made me ready that summer to sense some power within and beyond, it was freedom. I was free to be myself and to discover the world in a new way.

In my new freedom, I made a friend. At first I did not dare to believe it, but as the summer wore on, I realized it must be true. My friend lived two miles away by road, but only a half mile through the woods, and by the summer's end we had beaten a path through those woods and were constantly in each other's company.

It seemed as if nothing could go wrong that year I was ten. My friend already went to the new school, and when fall came I was no longer as fearful. I was shy and poor at my schoolwork, but I made other friends and slowly began to feel that all of life offered something of the joy and freedom I had felt in the woods and fields that summer. One day when I was visiting one of my new friends, her mother asked us to unpack a large crate. The crate contained family possessions, well protected by layers of good, old-fashioned wooden excelsior. We must have read Longfellow's poem "Excelsior" in school, because I knew that the other meaning of excelsior was "ever upward." "That's it!" I cried to my friend (with whom I had shared my atheistic convictions and my wonderings about that unexplained presence, the "Something" I sensed in the woods and fields). "We can call it X for excelsior!"

No matter how much happiness came to me that year, there still remained a dim background of fear: What if I said or did the wrong thing? Would these new friends cast me out? I was never quite sure. Then, when I was fifteen, I went to boarding school and in that strange, new place my fear returned.[3] It was not as strong and in time it receded, but it made me rebellious, and, in that rebellion, I adopted my parent's atheism. My fear made me want to prove that others were stupid and in that gently religious school, I lashed out at anyone foolish enough to take God seriously.

By the time I graduated, I was more at peace. Even my marks, which had always been low, had improved, but because my prior record was poor, I did not prepare for college.

"What do you want to do when you graduate?" asked my mother.

"I want to write," I replied, "but I think I need to do more living first. I'd like to go away somewhere and get a job."

But I had no idea what kind of a job or where.

"Why not try art school for a year?" said my mother.

And so, for want of another idea, I went to art school in the city of my childhood.[4]

The school had been founded to wed art and industry, and the students were drawn from a vast cross section of the population. Mill owners' children and mill workers' children took textile engineering. Second-generation immigrants did the same or took commercial art, photography, or architecture. Painters and sculptors from many backgrounds plunged into their work with passionate intensity and lived Bohemian lifestyles. Everyone was different, and difference was the norm. If difference was the norm, then I did not have to worry about conforming. For the first time in my life, fear completely dropped away, and I was tremendously happy. I decided to major in painting and I stayed four years.

As a young adult I seldom thought about God, and if the subject arose, I would say I was an atheist. I no longer felt the need to lash out and try to make people feel stupid, but I did enjoy the intellectual challenge of an argument with a believer. Nor did I think much about the X of my childhood, although at times I still had a sense of an unexplained presence. Sometimes it came upon me in the midst of conversation with a friend, sometimes when I was alone, and often while I was painting. If I had thought further, I might have related some of these perceptions to X. But not to God. God, in my mind, was only a subject for intellectual argument.

2. The Kingdom of God

Believing in God means getting down on your knees.

MARTIN LUTHER

God did not become a conscious reality in my life until I was thirty-one. By then I was happily married, had three children, and lived in a small suburban town.[1]

My husband and I had very different personalities. I was quiet and introspective, while he came on larger than life. It was not that he was tall, but he laughed and cried, talked and argued, worked and played with his whole being. In spite of these differences, we had much in common. We loved books and gardening and art, and we wove these into the pattern of our days. There was also a deep desire to do what we could to leave the world a better place than we found it. Over the years, we joined in many efforts to help both individuals and institutions, but from the first our most serious commitment was to work for peace. World War II had recently ended, and the specter and prophecy of Hiroshima and Nagasaki haunted us.

My husband, too, had been scarred in childhood. His father ignored him and his mother was a tremendously strong-willed person with extremely high ideals of perfection for herself and everyone else. Our scars left us with blind spots and inadequacies, and our marriage was not always easy. Nor were we the best of parents. But we cared about each other, the children, and the larger world, and an innate sense of good will helped us through the rough spots. Such serious reflections, however, did not often cross our minds in the early years of marriage.

We were survivors, we were young and in love, and the war was over.

We had bought a small Cape Cod house, one of twenty on a dead-end street. The road was ideal for children. There were children on tricycles and bicycles, children pulling wagons, children tumbling in the fall leaves or sliding down the hill in winter. Our society was one of commuters, mothers, and children or, as William Whyte described development living, "a dormitory with babies."

Back in those days, few women felt cheated out of careers, and I certainly did not. My life was full and I was content. I did, however, sometimes get bored doing housework and amused myself by puzzling over larger philosophical thoughts while doing dull jobs. One day I fell to thinking about being an atheist. I remember that I was shaking a mop out the back door when I suddenly realized that *atheist* was not exactly the right word to describe my beliefs.

"An atheist," I said to myself, "is sure that God doesn't exist. But I'm not *sure*, so I must be an agnostic."

I was utterly surprised! Why hadn't I ever stopped to realize this before?

I gave the mop a final shake and stood in the kitchen thinking. I didn't like the idea of being an agnostic. To say "I don't know" about something as basic as whether God exists or not was unsettling. How could one base one's life on an uncertainty?

I decided to read ten books on religion and see what they said. Ten was a nice round number and enough to make it a serious—but not too daunting—quest. I went to the town library, found the section on religion, and looked at the books on the shelves. I didn't know where to start, so my choices were almost random. There was a history of Islam, I remember, a book on comparative religion, and something by a Christian missionary in India. None of them seemed to speak to my question. I found an old Bible in the house and read it from cover to cover, but it didn't help either.

I had expected something else. What was it? It did not occur to me that that something had anything to do with X. I still did not equate X with God. X had been a doorway in my childhood, a doorway into an expanded world. And more than a doorway, X was somehow a part of that expanded world where freedom, friendship, creativity, and love brought me from the prison of childhood into a full and happy life. But God? God was an intellectual idea surrounded by strange stories and improbable events. At least that was the impression the books gave me. They seemed flat, dull, strange, and not in the least connected with my life.

I had read about seven books and was dutifully still reading, even though I had inwardly given up, when I thought of another plan. Somewhere, in the Bible or another book, I had read, "The Kingdom of God is within you."[2]

"Do you suppose," I reflected, "that they mean it literally?"

I decided to find out. "I'll look," I thought, "this afternoon when the children are taking their naps."

When the house was quiet, I went to our bedroom, closed the door, and sat down in a comfortable chair. I remember that I felt as if I were clearing a space in the room of my mind and throwing out extraneous clutter.

When my mind seemed reasonably empty, I paused. It was very still. "There's nothing here," I thought.

And then I realized that I was wrong. God was there. And I knew somehow that God had been there all along if I had only bothered to look.

I did not immediately equate God and X—that came when I had time to reflect. But the God of this inner kingdom was not the intellectual concept I had argued against, but a living presence.

I went around in a daze for the rest of the day. There had been nothing dramatic about my experience, no vision, no voice of God. It was very quiet. Yet at the same time, I had a sense of vast change.

I know now that every lasting conversion is a turning. You are going in one direction, and then you turn and start going in another. All I knew then was a desire to respond. "Surely," I said to myself, "I shouldn't just keep on with life as usual. . ."

But what could I do? The pattern of my days was set. There seemed little scope or time for anything else.

I remember the next morning looking out the living room window to the turnaround circle on our dead-end street. Our two older children were there with several friends, two mothers with baby carriages, and a miscellaneous jumble of dogs, small children, and tricycles. In a minute or so I would join them, but the baby was still asleep. I stood there, holding her snow-suit, and thought about my life.

I saw no dramatic changes I could make. A volunteer activity or so and a bit of reading were all the extras I had time for.

"What do you expect me to do, God?"

"You could pray."

Was I talking with myself? Or was that God's idea? I didn't know. But it was the only idea I had. In any case, it would have to wait until tomorrow. The baby had woken up.

It is not easy, or at least it was not easy for me, to find the time to pray. "Now look," I told myself sternly when several days had somehow gone by, "just start with ten minutes a day." But there was always something more "important" to do: an overdue letter to write, the messy linen closet to sort. I would do those first and before I knew it, my bit of free time was up and I had forgotten to pray. But slowly, over many months, I built a habit. Ten minutes a day became fairly regular and some-times it became fifteen minutes or even thirty. Since I had no church affiliation and no preconceived idea of what or how I should be praying, I learned to pray by praying. My prayers were very simple. I talked with God about how to become a better person. If I couldn't make any big changes in my life, perhaps, with God's help, I could make small ones.

There was one big difference between my childhood conception of X and my present feelings about God. It had never occurred to me that I could talk with X, but here I was, holding conversations with God as with a friend. Prayer, I discovered, was a very companionable business. It was a matter of talking about joint projects, a variety of campaigns to help me become more nearly the person both God and I desired. Sometimes we would work on my trying to really *listen* to people, to pay attention to their words and to grasp the ideas and feelings behind their words. Sometimes I was to concentrate on the children. "Just relax," God might say, "and take more time to play with them." After a few weeks of such a campaign, God would draw my attention to something else. "Count your blessings," God would say. "Every day, think of what you are grateful for."

A typical campaign would go something like this: "Well, God," I would say, "what next?" And somehow, either in the silence, through the words of my better self, or in the slowly changing content of my own prayer to God, I would sense an answer.

"Yes, I agree," I might say. "I haven't done very well in trying to be more patient with my exasperating friend, but I don't know what to do."

And then I would sense the reply, "You could pray for her."

The answer surprised me. I had heard of praying for people who were sick, but my friend was not sick. However, I'd received my answer and I responded, "All right, God, I'll try."

And so, day after day for several weeks, I prayed for my friend. I held her up to God and thought about her. I began to see her difficulties. "Give her strength, God."

I saw good sides of my friend that I had ignored and found myself thanking God for them. I understood so much more about her that I had the feeling that she was becoming almost transparent to me. I was, of course, very far from understanding her that well, but I certainly understood her better than I had before.

Downtown shopping I suddenly ran into my friend and I was so startled it must have shown on my face. She smiled and said, "You look like you've seen a ghost."

"Sorry!" I exclaimed. "I'd just been thinking about you and wondering how you were."

"Really?" she asked.

"Yes, really," I replied.

And then, perhaps the next day, God would somehow suggest a whole new campaign.

These campaigns did not usually end in victory. Sometimes there was improvement, but a bigger change was in awareness. I became more aware of others, of myself, of God, and of limitless horizons of love and learning. There was, for instance, the word *redemption*. Christians kept using the word, but I didn't understand it. "Redeemed?" I thought. "Redeemed from what?" I felt back in the Garden and God was in charge. All I had to do was to ask God's help and do my bit to be a better wife, mother, friend, and citizen. What did "redemption" have to do with it?

I don't remember how often I had to fail in my small efforts to be a better human being before my perspective began to change. All I had to do was "do my bit," but I could not do it. Oh, perhaps I improved here and there, but for the most part I failed. Not just once or twice, but time and time again. There it was in St. Paul: For the good that I would do I do not, and the evil that I do not want, I do. How well I understood that! But St. Paul understood redemption when he wrote that, and I did not.

In the beginning God often called me away from one campaign and into another before I'd seemed to have gotten much of anywhere with the first. Many months later we would go back to the first and try again only to leave it unfinished also after several weeks of work. For a year or so I had no sense of failure. God seemed to change the subject before I had to face failure. But eventually these recurring campaigns with little or no improvement began to bother me. I grew impatient with myself. And if I was impatient, how about God? God seemed to be asking such little things of me.

"Surely," I thought, "if I could not even do as God wished in small things, then God would lose patience with me. Was I to lose all the joy I had gained?" I felt a wave of fear.

One campaign I had fought so often it bored me was not eating between meals. I didn't particularly need to diet, but I didn't need extra food either. My life was very comfortable, and there were hungry people in the world. "You're quite right," said God. "Let's try again."

That day was little different than a hundred others except perhaps that I had more resolve. I got up from my knees and went about my daily tasks. Three hours later, in the very act of absentmindedly eating the third of three crackers with peanut butter, I remembered.

None of the other failures had bothered me greatly. I'd just said, "I'm sorry, God," and gone on, but this overwhelmed me. It was such a *little* thing of God to ask of me, and my resolve had been so clear and strong such a short time before. But beside that, the repeated failures and the fear of losing God had been building. "God could not possibly have this much patience."

I went to my room, fell on my knees, and turned to God in all the truth of my inner thoughts and feelings. I don't think I said a word, but just knelt there in despair. And then, suddenly—and again without words—night turned to day. It was as if a door in a dark cellar had been flung open on a sunlit spring orchard. Joy returned. God was there, and I knew somehow that it was all right.

Even after this experience I was slow to realize that it related to the word *redemption,* but when I did, the word came to life. "What are we redeemed from?" I asked myself. "Ourselves. We can't make it alone. But we have to try, and then God will make up the difference between who we were created to be and what we've done with the raw material."

Without realizing what I was doing, I was slowly building a relationship with God. In those first years of prayer I didn't think very much about this. I was caught up in the present reality. It was years later, when I began to try to help others to learn to pray, that I felt the need to understand the process more clearly. Looking back on my own experience and thinking about what was happening to the people I was trying to help, I saw certain common patterns. Among other things, I realized that the building blocks of this relationship consist of what you and God do together and what you learn about God and yourself in the process. In this it is little different than any human relationship. Yet it obviously *is* different. You are not talking to someone across the table but to someone within and yet beyond you. Someone with whom you feel at ease and yet someone who makes you feel like falling on your knees.

My suburban family life held nothing unusual, nothing adventurous. In contrast, my growing relationship with God held horizons beyond imagining. Day after day, new vistas opened, new paths lay before me. Yet these paths were through the thickets of everyday life rather than in distant jungles, and the vistas were familiar territory put in a new light by God. Yet this just increased the wonder of it. At one and the same time to be conscious of God as the Creator of the world who upheld the stars and as the Companion who talked with me about the trifles of daily life was staggering. But somehow I didn't doubt it, for everything in my life had begun to be seen from a different perspective.

Besides praying, I often just thought about God. With wonder, I realized that my childhood perception of X as being in every leaf and tree was true of God. But God was not just in nature, God was in me. And if God was in me, then God was in everyone. Riding in an elevator, I would suddenly remember this and look in wonder at a fellow passenger. That stodgy-looking woman with many parcels. Did she know? No matter. God knew. I felt joyous, lighthearted in the knowledge.

I also realized the truth of my childhood understanding of X in another way: I did not see God as being solely in the world, as atoms or electricity are in the world. God was greater than the world, beyond the world as well as within it. "God," I thought, "is either GOD, or God is not. The whole point is that it is GOD within you, within the stodgy woman in the elevator, within the sassafras leaf."

To me, as I grew in my relationship with God, this all seemed as natural as breathing. I was back in the Garden of Eden I had found when I was ten, but the whole world was now the Garden.

For the four years following my conversion, my inner world was increasingly full of joy and adventure. I felt like shouting from the rooftops for sheer exuberance. But in fact, for three of those years, I spoke to no one about God, not even to my husband. The self-styled atheism that had so recently been mine had been either a weapon or an intellectual plaything. This was deeply personal, and I had no desire to talk about it. It was a year or more before I even began to go to church.

"There are others, you know," said God.

"Others?"

"Other people who know me," said God. "It's important for you to be with them."

I felt a sinking feeling. "They'll meet me on the way in and say, 'I thought you were an atheist.' I wouldn't know what to say."

"I'll be with you," said God.

And so I began to go to church.[3] No one ever stopped me and said, "I thought you were an atheist." Perhaps they'd forgotten.

Church was not completely strange to me because of the three years I had spent in that gently religious boarding school. Religious instruction had not been obligatory, but we did have to go to church and to daily chapel. As it was an Episcopal school, I therefore became familiar with Episcopal services. It was now comforting to have something familiar, and so I began to attend the nearby Episcopal church. I still wasn't sure I was a Christian. And if I was a Christian, which kind was I? The denominations seemed to hold different beliefs. How could all of them be true? Yet, how could only one be true?

I began to read again. I looked up different religions and denominations and soon found that religions other than Christianity posed more problems for me than Christianity. We live in a Christian culture and atheist or not, I had been exposed to images, stories, and ways of thinking that made Christianity more understandable than Hinduism, Buddhism, or Islam. But all of the Christian denominations seemed to have formal patterns of belief and this concerned me. There was a deep simplicity about my belief in God, and I did not want to have to force it into a pattern.

I tried other churches, but in the end I stayed with the Episcopal church. Episcopalians recited the historic creeds and these were very strange to me, but they did not seem to threaten to impose a tightly woven structure of belief. They were more like a song or a poem, and I decided not to worry about the creeds for a while. Episcopalians seemed more concerned with *worship* than with intellectual understandings of God. The people got down on their knees and prayed. And, although I still spoke to no one about God, the presence of these other worshipers as I worshiped began to become important to me.

For two more years, I kept on praying at home and in church without ever discussing my new beliefs with anyone but God. Life continued to be an unbelievably joyous adventure. I had thought I was happy before I had found God, but I hadn't known what happiness meant.

It was now three years after my conversion. "Aren't you ever going to get baptized?" asked God.

"Well, I'd like to, but then I'd have to believe what the creeds say about you. I'm not sure that I do."

"What bothers you?" asked God.

"Well, mostly that bit about the only son of God. That seems insulting to other religions."

"When you think about Christ, what seems most important to you?"

I paused and thought. "Well, I guess it's that you came to earth as a human being. I mean, Jesus was human, and nothing was easy, but you were in Jesus and he did what you said."

"Why is that so important to you?"

"Because it showed us the way. We aren't supposed to just imagine you in heaven. We are supposed to find you inside us and inside other people and everywhere."

"I think that's enough for now," said God. "Do you want to join the church?"

"Yes, please," I said very quietly. "But do I believe enough?"

"Stop worrying," said God.

And so I went to see the rector about baptism. I felt terribly shy and awkward as I tumbled out my story and asked if I could be baptized, but I can remember that he kept smiling as I talked and I wondered why. Now that I know something of all the misery that people bring to a minister's office, I see why. My story was a welcome change. He asked a few questions and said, "Yes, you may be baptized."

Several days later, with my husband and a Christian friend as witnesses, I was baptized.

3. Sacrament

Sacraments as such tell us little or nothing. . . . They do some-
thing. They communicate "otherness" . . . through things—
concrete, natural things.

EVELYN UNDERHILL

Both intellectually and emotionally my baptism was even quiet-
er than my conversion. It felt like a simple assent to something
long true. But in the following weeks and months, I realized
that I had a different feeling when I went to church or even
when I drove past the church and looked up at the steeple and
the cross. I was a part of this. It was my home.

I still spoke very little about my inner feelings. But Sunday
after Sunday I found my horizons broadened and my faith nurtured simply by being a Christian among Christians. The common words of prayer, carrying the diverse but related thoughts
of hundreds of kneeling people, spoke to me even as I prayed.
Somehow, without anyone talking of them, my understanding
of phrases of the prayers, canticles, and hymns grew deeper
and broader as I joined in that wonderful, soaring rumble of
common prayer prayed out loud.

If I had followed the usual Christian pattern, I would have
been baptized as a baby and confirmed in my early teens, but I
found that I was glad that I had become a Christian as an adult.
Everything about Christianity was sparkling fresh and new.
Understanding did not always come easily, but the search for
answers was never dull.

"There are confirmation classes for adults," said the rector,
"but the classes and confirmation itself are not for several
months. You became a Christian at baptism and you may par-

ticipate in the sacrament of Holy Communion, the Eucharist, without waiting for confirmation."

But I wanted to wait. Everything was moving too fast for me. I didn't really understand what had happened to me in baptism and I certainly didn't understand the Eucharist.

Before I had decided on the Episcopal church, I had read books that compared the denominations. I found the sacraments of baptism and the Eucharist were a part of the belief and practice of almost every Christian denomination, but that they were given very different interpretations and emphases. Even the name of the service commemorating Christ's last supper before his crucifixion is, I learned, variously called the Lord's Supper, Holy Communion, and the Eucharist. Some denominations, like the Roman Catholic, give tremendous importance to sacraments. Others, like the Baptist, pay more attention to the Bible, preaching, and spontaneous prayer. The Episcopal church, I found, was positioned somewhere in the middle.

Eager as I was to learn, I discovered that the sacraments did not fit into a neat pattern of understanding. I liked the traditional definition: *A sacrament is an outward and visible sign of an inward and spiritual grace*[1] (so, for instance, the use of water is an outward and visible sign that God does something spiritual in the sacrament of baptism). I learned that grace meant the unearned gift of God, and I liked that definition too. But to try to define God's gift and the human action in a sacrament, to describe and encompass them, felt impossible. To talk about sacraments seemed at one and the same time to be talking of something infinitely large (as large as God) and something very small (a drop of water, a sip of wine, a fragment of bread). The whole idea seemed open to a thousand interpretations.

"Was I supposed to choose between these interpretations?" I asked the rector.

"No. You may have them all if you want."

I guessed that was what I wanted.

The day of confirmation came. The bishop laid his hands on my head and spoke to God of "this thy child, Avery," and it was done.

The "laying on of hands" as performed in the confirmation service[2] is, I had learned, described twice in the Bible in the book of Acts.[3] In both descriptions after the disciples laid their hands on people, they "received the Holy Spirit." Earlier in Acts the coming of the Holy Spirit to the disciples is described: They were gathered in one place praying, and suddenly the Spirit came to each of them "like tongues of fire."[4]

I certainly did not feel "tongues of fire" when the bishop laid his hands on my head any more than I had felt anything at my baptism. In both cases, I said yes to God before witnesses. Was that all that was supposed to happen? On the other hand, I knew that I was not the same person I had been three years before. Something had definitely happened to me, but it had happened before I was either baptized or confirmed. If it was not the Spirit, then I didn't know how to describe it. These questions and confusions did not deeply trouble me. At the very least, baptism and confirmation symbolized and sealed what had already happened. "God," I thought, "is not a captive of time."

The first job I was asked to do for our church was to help sort out the library, which was a jumble of new and old books. I'd never thought before about what makes a book a classic until I sorted those books. There were books written ten years before that seemed dated. There were others written fifty years earlier that seemed as valid as when they were written. Among the latter were several books by Evelyn Underhill, that remarkably learned British laywoman who died in 1941. I had never heard of her before, but I sat on the library floor amid a pile of books entranced by what I had found. In one of her books I read the words I quoted at the beginning of this chapter: "Sacraments as such tell us little or nothing. . . . They do something. They communicate 'otherness' . . . through things—concrete, natural things."

I felt tremendously excited when I read those words. Somehow this was related to X in a sassafras leaf, a blade of grass, a human being. Otherness—God—is in everything, and sacraments communicate otherness. Priest and people hold up concrete, natural things to God and God says, "Yes, I am here." And we celebrate it and God is communicated.

The sacrament of Holy Communion, or the Eucharist, communicated Otherness to me from the start. I could not describe it, but this did not trouble me. At some deep and wordless level, I knew that it was a *belonging*. I belonged to Christ; Christ belonged to me; I belonged on my knees and in the midst of this kneeling congregation.

As months passed, the repeated words and actions of the Communion service began to echo in mind as well as heart. There were, I discovered, layers upon layers of meaning, all of them windows to God's landscape. Sometimes one meaning would stand out for me and sometimes another. One day I would be caught up in wonder at the thought that Jesus and his friends were gathered around the table and that we were there too. On another day I would be particularly conscious that the supper was on the evening before crucifixion. "Do this," said Jesus, with cup in hand, "in remembrance of me."[5] Words would echo in my mind and lead to others: "Do this. Drink this cup of suffering, of companionship, of the loneliness of death, of compassion, of victory."

The denominations argue over exactly how Christ is present in the sacrament, but to me it seems a foolish argument. Christ is present. Christ is already in the world and in us, waiting to be recognized, accepted, followed. The sacrament, like a sudden light from heaven, illuminates the Truth and offers Christ to us.

More and more there were times of thanksgiving. *Eucharist*, I learned, means "thanksgiving." There I was, feeling all scattered, pressured, sinful. Slowly the holy rhythms of the service would center me and God would come through. Otherness would communicate through consecrated bread and wine. I would be blessed, know that I was whole again, and be filled with thanksgiving.

One of the things I learned about baptism, the earliest of Christian sacraments, is the traditional Christian belief that when nothing else is possible, a layperson may baptize someone. One day I opened my newspaper and read a report of a lay baptism. A young man and woman had been swimming in the surf when the man was suddenly attacked by a shark. He called to his companion to swim for shore. She started to do so, thought better of it, and swam to rescue her friend. She managed to pull him to shore, but he was obviously so terribly mutilated he could not live. Kneeling beside him in the sand, she asked whether he wished to be baptized. He gasped out a yes and she baptized him with sea water.[6]

On reading and remembering this story, my heart turns over and I make an interior assent to the man's dying wish, the woman's offer, and God's grace.

"But what," I asked myself, "about infant baptism? A baby cannot understand and so cannot assent. Is infant baptism anything more than a nice custom and a promise by parents and godparents to bring up the child as a Christian? Because if it's nothing more, we have left out God's action, there is no grace, and it is not a sacrament."

In the parish library I had discovered the novels of Charles Williams, and it was in reading and reflecting on one of his novels that my puzzling over infant baptism came to a resolution.[7] Williams's novels are full of struggles between spiritual forces of good and evil. One young woman, caught up in a web of evil, dreams of water and this seems to give her the strength she needs to break free. Later in the book she finds out that when she was a baby, her nurse had been disturbed that her charge was not to be baptized and secretly baptized the child herself.

It did not matter to me that Williams's story was fiction. It challenged me to answer the question: Does infant baptism of itself, discounting being brought up as a Christian, in some way change a person? Was the balance for good or evil within the baby in Williams's story somehow weighted more toward good when earthly words and water and an invisible action of God claimed the child as Christ's? Or is infant baptism just a sentimental time of wishing the new human being well? I decided that it was more than that. Somehow, otherness is communicated and God's grace touches the child in a way that is deeper than words and beyond definition.

Sacraments are not necessarily limited to baptism and the Eucharist. Various denominations, I had learned, recognize different numbers of them. Confirmation, for instance, is sometimes considered a sacrament and sometimes not. Marriage may also be seen as a sacrament, as may confession and the ordaining of priests. But how many sacraments there were didn't concern me because I began to see how wide and all-embracing the whole idea was.

I remember a particular time when my understanding of sacraments had both deepened and broadened. I had been in church. I was standing in the midst of the congregation, and the bread and wine were being brought to the altar for the celebration of the Eucharist. They were not consecrated yet and so were not supposed to be anything but bread and wine. Yet I suddenly realized that they stood for something. We had taken what God had given us—wheat and grapes—and made them into bread and wine. In like manner, we had taken the lives given to us by God and made them into their present form. That bread and wine stood for my life, everyone's lives, the world's life. They were a sign of everything for which we were thankful, for which we were sorry, for which we wept. Our hopes, our joys, our sins, our stupid mistakes, those we loved, those we hurt, our families, our friends, our enemies, our weaknesses—all these and more were symbolized by the bread and wine. And then they were offered at the altar. They were taken into Christ, accepted, blessed, transformed.

This vision, these layers of meaning not only gave me a deeper appreciation of the meaning of the sacraments of the church, but also gave me a way of seeing all life as potentially sacramental. I found that when I offered anything I happened to be doing to God, as the bread and wine were offered, it became something beyond itself. "Here, God" I said as I set the table for dinner, "this is for you." When I drove the car or weeded the garden or washed the dishes, I tried to remember to offer these acts also. And I realized that when I did so, I acted for a moment as a priest, celebrating God's presence in the ordinary things of life.

4. A Guide

If you have sought a spiritual companion before, you know the ambivalence it can involve. Whom can I really trust with this most intimate dimension of my being?

TILDEN EDWARDS

It was almost a year after my baptism that I felt the first intimations that a slow change was taking place within me. Increasingly, God, who had seemed so very near and accessible, seemed far away and out of reach. In time this became constant, and the joy that I had felt for so long dimmed and then was gone. I prayed, but it meant nothing. It was just my voice echoing in the fog.

Although the change was gradual, it was vast. Everything in life had seemed fraught with meaning, with possibilities, with hope. And now it was gone.

What had happened? Where was God? Why had I lost the joy I had found? I had no idea. I searched my mind for answers, but I found none. Hesitantly I asked a few Christian friends if they had ever felt like this.

"Oh, yes," they answered, "we all have times when God seems distant. It will pass."

I doubt if I gave them any real idea of the contrast between where I had been and where I was. My deep feelings about God were locked in an inner room and I only shared fragments of these feelings with others in conversations.

Weeks and then months passed with no change. Finally, I realized that I must find help. I had to unlock that inner room to someone who could understand and tell me what to do. But to whom could I go?

One person kept returning to my mind. She was a professor at a seminary in the city whom I had met just once some months earlier. I wasn't sure why I believed that she could help me, but I did. Yet every time I thought of going to see her, I was engulfed with hesitation. Was this really what I was supposed to do?

Both the world and I have changed a great deal in the twenty-five years or so that have passed since I faced this dilemma. At that time spirituality and prayer were never mentioned among my friends and neighbors and seldom mentioned among my new Christian companions. Prayer seemed to be a subject for monks and nuns, or resorted to in moments of desperation. To speak then of experiences of prayer as deep as mine had been felt peculiar, and I did not do peculiar things easily in those days. To go into the city to talk to a comparative stranger about such matters seemed very peculiar indeed.

I became ensnared in ambivalence: Was I just lacking in courage? Was I conceited to think that I needed an expert? Was this a wise idea or misguided?

My own prayers, which had made so many choices clear for me, were no longer of help, but I persisted. Day after day, I spoke to the God I could no longer hear. But the darkness remained impenetrable. Three months of indecision went by and the ambivalence was making me feel worse. Finally, I realized that I had to decide. With a brief prayer of committal to whatever God had in mind, I reached for my Bible and opened it at random. The first words that met my eyes were "They were like sheep without a shepherd." That was enough. I needed a shepherd.

I wrote to the Professor: "I seem to be very confused and need someone to talk to. Could I come to see you?" She replied, "Of course," and set a date.

The seminary where the Professor taught was housed in a group of Victorian buildings in the city. They formed a quadrangle around an oasis of trees and grass crisscrossed with paths between the various buildings.

I was early for my first appointment with the Professor, and I sat on a bench in the close, as it was called. The seminarians still wore gowns in the 1950s and I watched them hurrying to classes holding armfuls of books, their open gowns flapping behind them. I was glad to be distracted as I was feeling very keyed up and a bit frightened.

I looked at my watch. Yes, it was time now. I walked down the path and found the building the Professor had described. I went in, knocked on her door, and waited for the unknown.

The Professor greeted me warmly and took me into her book-lined study. "Now you just sit there," she said, "while I get our lunch."

I stared at the books hungrily, for I still believed books held answers even though I had not found the right ones.

Over lunch and after, I told her where I had been and where I was. From time to time she nodded, asked a question, or added a comment. For the most part she was silent, yet her few words and even her nods, told me that I had come to the right place. She seemed to find nothing strange about my story. Indeed, she indicated that I was on a journey that many had traveled before me. I no longer felt "peculiar." I felt that I had come home.

When I had written to the Professor, I had not only asked if I could see her, but if I could come back from time to time. When she was talking about my returning for another visit, the Professor used the words *spiritual direction.*

"What does that mean?" I asked.

She looked surprised that I did not know. "I think it's what you asked for," she replied gently. "Your letter sounded as if you wanted someone to guide you on your spiritual journey. Is that what you'd like?"

"Yes, please. But I've never heard it called spiritual direction."

"Having a spiritual director, a spiritual guide, is a very old Christian tradition," she said.

I felt astounded. This was what I needed and yet I had never heard of it. "I am glad that I found you," I said.

The fog that had bound my days for months lifted soon after I went to the Professor and I felt back in touch with God. It was as if God had been waiting for me to take action. Certainly without those empty months I would never have gone to the Professor, and the decision to seek her help was one of the major turning points in my life. Not only did the Professor guide me on my journey, but she introduced me to our Christian heritage of teachings on prayer, a treasure house of which I had previously known nothing. Here, among ancient writings and modern writings I found both confirming echoes of all that I had experienced and new ways of prayer and living.

The first and most basic thing I learned from the Professor and her books was about a *rule of prayer*. "You mean like monks and nuns have a *rule?*" I asked in surprise.

The Professor laughed. "Yes, they have rules too, but you don't need one like that. Tell me," she asked, "what sort of prayers do you pray regularly—'as a rule?'"

"Oh," I replied, "so *that's* what it means."

And so we went through, for the first of many times, those ways of prayer that were an ordinary part of my life, and the Professor commented and suggested additions and changes. For instance, she pointed out that the service of Morning Prayer in the *Book of Common Prayer* was not just meant for use in church on Sunday, but at home every day. "This," said the Professor, "is *corporate* prayer. Even when you are physically alone, you are spiritually praying with other Christians, Christians who are praying these prayers today and Christians who have prayed them down the centuries."

It was a heady thought. "I'd like to try it," I said.

I met with the Professor every two or three months, but we exchanged letters every week. "Morning Prayer," I wrote, "is going well. Repeating some of those old prayers and canticles day after day makes them come alive. But I also get very confused by all this stopping and looking things up. It's disruptive. I mean there I am, praying along, with the prayers saying things for me and to me and with me, and then I have to stop and look up the special prayer for the week or the Bible readings for the day."

The Professor wrote back with practical suggestions about using bookmarks and looking things up before I started. The process gradually improved, although absentminded confusions about what to read next have remained with me to this day. There was, however, something much deeper about Morning Prayer that came through to me in spite of the confusions about sequence. It was as if all the people who originally wrote and prayed the prayers and all those who had prayed them since were a present and living choir. If I felt low, distracted, or unable to pray well on my own, there they were, "a cloud of witnesses."

Conversations with the Professor were not, however, confined to what kind of prayers I prayed as a rule. We also discussed their meaning. I remember, for instance, talking to her about sensing the presence of God in people, in nature, in the midst of everyday life, and finding myself suddenly praying. She nodded her head as I spoke and then said, "Yes. You have a natural bent toward the *via positiva*, toward worshiping God in and through the world. But there is also the *via negativa*, and you must keep a balance. In the negative way you look at an object, a situation, or a person and say to yourself, 'That isn't God.' And you pray to the God beyond."

As long as the Professor talked of prayer or gave me books to read about prayer I was happy. But then she began to give me books on theology and I was miserable. They seemed heavy, dead. Prayer was light, alive, moving. Why were theology and prayer so different? The Professor insisted. "Have you read that book I gave you yet?" she would write in a letter. And then she would change to the red ribbon on her typewriter, "You *must* read it."

And so I did. I read that one and other books of theology, but always, in those first years, I had to discipline myself to read them. I bridled when the text seemed to make Christianity seem too narrow. I yawned when the words seemed long and turgid. I grew impatient when I thought the author's thinking didn't make sense. But I read them.

I knew, of course, that theology means "our knowledge of God," and it was to God I prayed. But the God to whom I prayed did not make me yawn.

It did not occur to me at first that the knowledge of God I gained through prayer was also theology, but a real turning point in my attitude toward theology came one day when the Professor was talking about transcendence and immanence.

I didn't know the word *immanence*. "How do you spell it?" I asked.

"It *is* an awkward word," she replied. "It sounds like *eminence* or *imminence*. All it means is *inner*. When you see it spelled with a capital I, it refers to God's omnipresence in the universe. Immanence means that God is here, within us, within everything. And Transcendence, of course, means God beyond. Remember when we were talking of the *via positiva* and the *via negativa*? This is the theology at the base of those ways of prayer. Theology, you know, just means our knowledge of God."

And suddenly in my mind I was back in the Garden of my childhood where I had sensed, had *known*, in spite of my parents' beliefs, that there was *something* within and beyond. That, too, had been knowledge of God. This knowledge, this particular theology was confirmed for me now as an adult. When I looked at a leaf, a tree, a saintly person, a verse in the Bible, or the stodgy woman in the elevator and found in them signs of God, my heart would leap in response. But even as that happened, I knew the contradiction. God was within them, but God was not solely in them—God was also beyond.

It was one thing to have felt as a child that *something*, X, was within and beyond. It was yet another to have the realization in my adult years that X was God, within me, within others, and abroad in the world. But to learn that I was far from alone in this realization, that it was a basic Christian doctrine, gave it a whole new dimension. If this was what theology was all about, then theology was worth a bit of attention.

By "attention" I didn't necessarily mean studying difficult books—although by now I was studying them. It was *thinking* about God that excited me, not thinking in an ivory tower, but thinking in the world, in the midst of life. It was also thinking that was never far from prayer. There seemed to be a whole way of looking at theology from the perspective of prayer. It was still theology, but it was more personal, more generous, more alive.

As time went on, I found that this mixture of prayer, theology, and everyday life was often a heady brew. I remember one time a few days before Christmas when I read the words in a book now forgotten, "the Holy Child is born in our hearts." My thoughts soared. Idea tumbled after idea.

"The Holy Child is within us," I thought, "just waiting to be recognized, to be loved and nurtured."

I thought of the people I was to see that day and of others who came to mind unbidden. What could I see of the Child in them? In myself? How could I love and nurture the infant Christ?

These thoughts came and went during that particular day, right in the midst of the happy and quite secular mayhem of family Christmas preparations. First would come the remembrance "the Holy Child is born in our hearts." The thought would bring an inner leap of joy, of love of God. Then this would lead to love and prayer for whatever people came to mind. But then, almost instantaneously, I realized that I was thinking of a dimension of the Incarnation. God incarnate. God in a human being. I was back to my beloved Immanence. But was I? "This is not just Immanence," I said to myself, "Immanence is God everywhere. The Incarnation is God in one human being. Perfectly. The Holy Child is God incarnate. Yet the Holy Child is in all of us." Unconsciously, I used Mary's words to the angel, "How can this be?"[2]

But I did not feel like trying to figure out this holy puzzle. I only knew that it was true. My thoughts returned to my heart and, like the shepherds and kings, I adored the Holy Child.

As time went on, the inner gap in my mind between theology and prayer began to be bridged. The discovery that something that makes inner, living sense to you has been part of Christian practice and scholarly thinking for centuries is not only a confirmation of faith, it is like meeting an old friend in an unexpected place. You are filled with a delighted sense of recognition. After I began asking the Professor's help, this recognition happened often, either in reading books she had given me or in conversation.

I first went to the Professor in the fall of 1959. The next decade saw the rise of interest in Hinduism and Buddhism. Terms like *guru* and *zen master* began to appear frequently in books and articles, but I seldom heard reference to *spiritual directors*. Strange, I reflected. People were complaining about Christian practices being too restrictive and old-fashioned, and yet they could embrace the strict demands of Eastern religions. Gurus and zen masters seemed to ask complete obedience, whereas all the Professor did was turn to the red ribbon on her typewriter and insist I read a book.

I talked to the Professor about the nature of spiritual direction. She even thought the word *director* sounded too severe. It is more than being a teacher, she said. "God is in the relationship, you see. It's a triangle. You and I and God."

And I knew she was right.

5. Interlude in India

He who with intense longing weeps for God has found God.

RAMAKRISHNA

In one sense India has been more of a constant presence in my life than an interlude, but I have only been there once. It was for six weeks and fell between my first and second visits to the Professor.

My husband and I were deeply involved in a sister town relationship between our town and a town in India.[1] In the days when we began, there were few Indians in the United States, and a town friendship such as ours was rare. As a result, the friendship outgrew the bounds of one particular town and we welcomed people from all over India into our homes. Real friendships (as opposed to educational acquaintanceships) developed and lasted.

As I write these words, I hear a baby crying. She is the fourth generation of an Indian family I have been close to. When the child was to be born far from home and to a mother new to this country, I was asked to care for them for a few weeks. I said, "Of course."

"You must," they wrote me from India, "have been a member of our family in another incarnation." Yesterday I almost felt as if I was. The baby was twelve days old, and it was time for the traditional naming ceremony in which all the women of the family whisper the baby's name in her ear and wish her well. It was also the second day of Divali, the Festival of Lights, when Hindus celebrate the victory of good over evil. "Surely, we should celebrate," I thought.

The young mother agreed, so I asked those close to us to come by that evening, and we spent the day cooking a festive dinner. On one end of the dining table I placed all the candles I could find for the Festival of Lights. When the guests arrived, we lit them all and stood in front of the candles with the baby, who was happily mesmerized by the glow. We then handed her gently from one woman's arms to another's and each of us whispered the baby's name in her ear. It wasn't traditional to have the men join in at all, but we decided that they, too, should have a chance to wish the baby well, so each of us in turn wished the child happiness, health, friends, a peaceful world or whatever other wishes we felt in our hearts.

This relationship with India and Indians has been mine for over half of my life. I do not, of course, know the country well, nor am I an expert in any part of Indian culture, but something of that country, that culture, and the religion from which it springs has seeped into my heart and mind. I cannot think of suburban affluence, for instance, without remembering the young Indian girl crawling over the bit of barren ground by the ferry crossing in South India. She only had stubs for arms and legs but covered the ground with amazing speed when she saw that we were Western tourists. I asked our driver, "Would her parents have done that to her to make her a better beggar?"

"Of course," he replied.

The particularities of life make the generalities come alive. The "poverty of India" was no longer a textbook phrase. I found that the same was true of religion. I cannot think of reincarnation without remembering talking with a good Indian friend in my living room. We often talked of religion, and on this particular day I happened to mention praying for people who had died. "There is a prayer in our prayer book," I said, "about praying that people who have died 'go from strength to strength in a life of perfect service.'"

My friend looked startled. "You mean it's a Christian belief that people can grow closer to God after they have died?"

"Well, I certainly believe it, and I think most Christians do," I replied.

A wonderful smile came over my friend's face, and with great relief in her voice, she said, "I'm *so glad*! I always thought you only had one chance."

I read books on Hinduism and found them dull and confusing. What was all this about realizing that the world was *maya* or illusion? It didn't feel like illusion to me.

I turned to the tales of Indian gods and goddesses and found them easier reading. But there was certainly nothing about these tales of heroes being rescued by flying monkeys and a young boy playing with milkmaids that made me think of God. They appealed to me as fairy stories appeal and no more.

Biography and autobiography were better. I read several biographies of Gandhi and had no doubt that he was a man close to God. I also read a life of Vinoba Bhave, Gandhi's disciple, entitled *India's Walking Saint*.[2] Vinoba walked from village to village persuading landowners to give land for those who had none. On the face of it, this was an impossible task. Even the richest in a village were incredibly poor. But Vinoba succeeded. He succeeded because the villagers were religious and Vinoba was obviously a saint.

"Every villager—man, woman, or child—is an incarnation of God's spirit," said Vinoba. "You are all my Krishnas and I have come to worship you."[3]

Once a widow fell at his feet, saying, "A relative of my husband's has seized my acre of land."

Vinoba spoke to the relative, who confessed his guilt, and then persuaded him to return the land. The really remarkable part of this incident is that the widow then offered the land to Vinoba. It is worth quoting at length:

The widow lived in one dark room, mud walls cracked and peeling because she had no cow and thus could not smear the cottage with the mixture of mud and cow dung that should be applied daily by every prudent Indian housewife. There was a clay pot with water in it, a flat iron frying pan, three tin lids, and a blackened hole in the mud floor which served as a cooking stove. The only piece of furniture was an old orange box and, in it, the widow's year-old babe born after her husband's death. Vinoba peered down and said: "Here is the Lord Krishna playing in his cradle." It was like a doctor saying: "This child has measles . . ." He spoke with no trace of sentiment.[4]

No matter how much this was an Indian and a Hindu story, it was easy for me to be moved by it. There was a universal holy quality about Vinoba and his work. His simplicity and directness reminded me of stories of Jesus.

My thoughts and feelings became more complex when I read Christopher Isherwood's biography of Ramakrishna.[5] Ramakrishna was a 19th-century Indian holy man with vast influence in India and beyond. His disciple, Vivekananda, brought Hinduism to the United States at the turn of the century. But fascinating as this history is, what caught my attention most and has remained in my mind all these years was Ramakrishna's devotion to Kali.

Of all Hindu gods and goddesses, it is Kali, the goddess of death, whose image seems furthest from God to the Western mind. It was easy for me to comprehend intellectually that Kali is worshiped because Hindus believe that without death one cannot move to the next incarnation, but the idea of worshiping God before one of Kali's images seemed incomprehensible to me. She is pictured as half demon and half emaciated hag. Her statues have garlands of skulls and are offered blood sacrifices.

Yet worship, devotion, and love of God—particularly through Kali—were utterly central for Ramakrishna. He was a Hindu saint, and his love of God radiated so surely from his presence that he attracted thousands of followers. Reading Isherwood's words, I too was moved. I still could not imagine worshiping Kali, but I had no doubt that through Kali, Ramakrishna was worshiping God, the same God I worshiped. His utter devotion, his love and grief, his longing for God came through and felt strangely familiar to me. "This could not be pagan aberration," I said to myself. "It was simply that we were both children of God and both loved God."

Yet reading the book still caused a shocking and confused jumble in my mind. "Some day, God, please help me to make sense of it."

I went to India a week ahead of my husband and stayed with Indian friends in Bombay. They were Brahmins, and I was their first non-Brahmin guest.

Waking early in the morning, I went out on the roofless porch off my room. From surrounding houses I heard prayers being said or chanted. Walking quietly downstairs in my bare feet, I almost tripped over the father of the household sitting cross-legged on the living room floor meditating.

What was I to make of this, young Christian that I was? Whether secretly or out loud, I could hardly even imagine the Christians in my hometown paying this much attention to prayer.

My young friend in the family and a friend of his took me on a train journey to Aurangabad to see the caves at Ellora and Ajanta. It was a night train, and we had to change at Manmad around one o'clock in the morning. There didn't seem to be any sense in trying to sleep before the change. "Look," I said, "why don't you try to explain Hinduism to me and I'll try to explain Christianity to you?"

And so, as the old steam train rattled through the night, we talked. I do not remember what we said, but I do remember a conviction that no matter how different our beliefs and our practices were, and they were very different, that God was still God. And God knew how it all fitted together even if we did not.

We were met in Aurangabad by a Parsee engineer, an employee of my friend's father. We climbed into his jeep and drove off to the caves. There we were met by a Moslem who was to be our guide.

I had seen photos of the famous cave paintings at Ajanta, but nothing had prepared me for the sculpture in the caves at El-lora. There, at different periods, Buddhists and Jains had carved monumental statues out of the living rock. Entering a dimly lit cavern, I slowly perceived a gigantic statue of Buddha towering before me. Was it just because we had been talking of God the night before that I felt so strongly the lingering effect of the past worship of thousands of people? Only in Chartres Cathedral had I felt this way before.

That night at dinner my friend asked me to say grace. The group at the table was made up of two Hindus, one Moslem, one Parsee, and myself, and we had spent the day in ancient Jain and Buddhist places of worship. I felt very much a Christian, but there was no way that I could negate, ignore, or belittle the past and present beliefs I had encountered that day.

"I'll do my best," I said.

The talking stopped and I prayed: "Lord of us all, be with us at this meal. May each of us in our own way sense your presence here and in the days to come and live as you wish us to live. We thank you for this day, this meal, and this companionship. Amen."

Much later in our journey my husband and I had dinner one night with an American who lived in India. He had made an extensive study of Hinduism, profound enough that he had been asked to give a paper before a scholarly Hindu society. We talked of religion, and I sensed that although he was very learned, his commitment was to intellectual knowledge rather than to God. "You can talk with Hindus about their beliefs," he said at one point, "but they will never mention their gurus to you."

I was startled. We had been traveling for several weeks, practically always in the company of Indian friends, and three of them had mentioned their gurus to me. I puzzled over this. I was a Christian and knew little of their religion, yet they instinctively felt closer to me and I to them. It must be, I decided, as if God were at the center of a sphere and people were on the outside. There were many ways into the center, but you had to choose a way. Going round and round the circle got you nowhere. Yet if two people were trying to reach God from opposite sides of the sphere, the closer they got to the center, the closer they got to God and each other.

I came home from India with three convictions: Many Hindus were closer to God (and therefore to Christ) than many Christians; Hinduism had a radically different set of beliefs about God from Christianity; and Hindu beliefs did not appeal to me, not only because they were so strange, but because they described matter as illusion and only God as real. "Christianity," Archbishop William Temple once said, "is the most materialistic of religions."

I agreed with him. Matter matters to Christians. God is real, but matter is real too, and God is in matter.

6. God and the Bible

When you read God's word, you must constantly be saying to yourself, "It is talking to me, and about me."

SØREN KIERKEGAARD

I returned from India ready, with the Professor's help, to learn more of Christianity. At that point, for example, I hardly knew the Bible.

Some people talk as if all you need to do to find God is to open the Bible and start reading. That certainly wasn't true for me. I read the Bible once through as a child, once as an adolescent, and once as an adult without it meaning much of anything to me. A growing relationship with God had to come first, and then the Bible began to come alive.

Although there are obvious disadvantages to having been brought up as an atheist, there are also distinct advantages. Everything about Christianity is fresh and exciting. I can remember one day buying J. B. Phillips's translation into modern English of the Acts of the Apostles.[1] I came home, sat down with my coat still on, and started to read. Two hours later, I had to tear myself away as the children were coming home from school. It was not, of course, just the translation. Acts is a book of action, an adventure story, and in modern English the action seemed to have happened just yesterday. As I sat there reading, that motley band of Jesus' friends walked straight into my living room. I saw them discouraged, bereft. I saw them obedient to the last words of their risen Lord, gathering in the upper room to wait and pray.[2] I saw them, in that same room, suddenly brought alive by the Holy Spirit and going forth in power to preach and heal in Christ's name. No one could have imagined the stories of those first disciples, and they were impossible to dismiss.

The kind of freshness I experienced reading the book of Acts in modern English was repeated for me in the Jerusalem Bible's version of the Old Testament, but from a vastly different perspective. Here the stories were far from seeming like newspaper accounts of recent happenings. They were ancient and they felt ancient. There was certainly historical reality in the Old Testament, but it didn't seem important to me at the time to figure out exactly what was factual and what was not. I just dove into that vast collection of books, letting it speak to me where it would. Yet I did wonder why so many of these strange and ancient stories seemed to have something to say to me. I certainly didn't think that the creation of the world or events in the Garden of Eden, for instance, had *happened* in the same sense that the stories of the apostles had happened. Not literally. Why then did they speak to me? I didn't know. But what was very obvious was that the ancient Israelites saw God not only as someone other, distant, and all-powerful, but as someone very much involved in the world. God was transcendent, awesome in majesty, yet God also told people how to live, was a part of their lives, and was with them in the roar of battle and in the "still, small voice." The God of Israel was clearly both immanent and transcendent.

I first grew to love the psalms in the *Book of Common Prayer*. The psalms *are* prayer and have been used as prayer by Jews and then by Christians for three thousand years. But they are not without an element of strangeness, because although some psalms have a peaceful and pastoral element, many are turbulent battlegrounds of conflicting passions. I sometimes think of the incongruous picture of a demure maiden in a more pious era clutching her small copy of the New Testament and the Psalms on her way to church. For whatever the psalms are, they are not demure, and three thousand years quickly fade as one is caught up in the strong feelings of the writer—love, hate, fear and joy. We see him repentant, reflective, pleading; we hear the psalms speak for the child, the saint, and the sinner within each of us. They wash over us like waves bringing the touch of God to all that is best and worst in our own hearts.

When I started reading the Bible, I preferred to read the Gospels in the beauty of the King James Version. Does it distance us from the real Jesus? Perhaps, but the writing in the New Testament is not just about a historical man, Jesus of Nazareth. It is about *God* in that human being. The problem is—and has always been—how to see Jesus as God while still seeing him as human. The beauty of Elizabethan English is like candles on the altar. It reminds us of who we are looking at.

There are times in the King James Version when the human reality of the scene breaks through the Elizabethan language. The Gospels are not purely spiritual, no matter how many candles you light. Certainly no one can read of Jesus stumbling under the weight of carrying the cross or later crying out from that same cross, "My God, my God, why hast thou forsaken me?"[4] without feeling the reality of it. This *happened* and we suddenly feel we are there. We feel both awe and identification. We have all stumbled under our cross and cried out to the God whose presence seems to have left us.

And dear Peter—how real he seems! If you ever think that the whole Bible is a fairy story (and who has not?), you doubt your doubts when someone as real as Peter steps forth from its pages in either Elizabethan or modern English. Impulsive and loving, meaning the best and failing, Peter touches a chord in all of us.

Although at first scenes of action in the Gospels were most compelling, I found that I was always moved by the parables of Jesus even when I did not understand them. I puzzled over this as I did over my reaction to the ancient Old Testament stories.

Many of the parables of Jesus are, I discovered, about the Kingdom of God. "The Kingdom of God is like . . ." they begin and go on to describe something little that caused great change and great joy. The Kingdom of God is like the leaven in the loaf,[5] the woman who lost a precious coin and found it,[6] the tiny mustard seed that grew into a huge bush.[7]

What is the "Kingdom of God?" I thought. The church? The way the world should be? Heaven? Israel under the Messiah? I learned from the Professor that Christian theologians speak of the Kingdom as *now* (Christ has come) and *not yet* (he will come again). And, indeed, some of Jesus' teachings refer to the Kingdom as present and some as future.

Jesus seldom explained a parable—"Let him who has ears, hear," he said.[8] As I read them, I found that I often could not avoid thinking about how it applied to my own life. Was this what Jesus meant about hearing?

The Kingdom of heaven is like a merchant seeking to buy pearls. When he found one pearl of great value, he went and sold all his possessions and bought it.[9]

I both yearned for that pearl and wondered if I would have the courage to sell all that I possessed to buy it. And then I would be comforted by:

The Kingdom of heaven is like a mustard seed which a man took and sowed in his field. It is a very small seed, but when it is grown becomes a great tree and the birds of the air rest in its branches.[10]

In my memory, my early random reading of the Bible and the way that I learned to read it from the Professor now blur in my mind. But I know that it was following her suggestion to say daily Morning Prayer with its accompanying Bible readings that made the Bible come alive for me.

Now, reading the Bible in the context of prayer is a vastly different matter from studying it with the aid of reference books. But it is also different, I found, from just sitting down and reading it like a novel (which was rather the way I had read the book of Acts). Yet even when I read the Bible like a novel, I realized that when I slowed down and let the words and images linger in my mind it sometimes seemed close to prayer.

Reading those appointed lessons slowly and in the middle of Morning Prayer caught them up in prayer, and they became prayer.

I doubt that I bothered to define the word *prayer* in those days, but I certainly saw it as something larger than asking God's help. In time, I grew to realize that prayer is any communication, any bond, between us and God. It is the substance and means of our relationship.

Saying Morning Prayer became a joyful habit. A quiet and regular time was not always possible so, if need be, I would take my prayer book and Bible with me on trips, to parking lots while waiting for a child, and to any quiet corner of the house in whatever time I could find.

The portions of the Bible appointed to be read each day were, I found, chosen and arranged with care. They represented the very core of the Bible. The ancient stories of the Old Testament, the prophets and psalms, the stories of Christ and his disciples, and the Letters of Paul and the others began to form a unified whole in my mind. Yet that was a minor gain compared to my learning to read the Bible as part of prayer.

I learned to listen while I read. Sometimes I would hear nothing except the words of my reading. More often, I was simply conscious that the passages were entering mind and heart and becoming part of me. But increasingly there were times when some aspect of what I was reading came home to me with such sudden strength and clarity that I was left with no doubt that God had something to say not just to the psalmist, the prophet, or the disciple—but to me.

I remember, for instance, reading in 1 Chronicles 13 the story of David and all Israel traveling with the ark of God, the symbol and center of their worship. Suddenly, the oxen pulling the cart on which the ark was traveling stumbled. A man called Uzzah, who was standing near, instinctively put out his hand to hold the ark steady. And God struck him dead.

If I had been reading with an intellectual approach, I would have had many questions about this quite horrifying story: Did

Uzzah really die or did some later writer invent his death to show how God thought people should think of the ark? Or did Uzzah coincidentally have a heart attack and people explained his death by the story? Or was God really that cruel? I would have also wanted to know a great deal about the Israelites' attitude toward the ark.

But I wasn't *studying* the passage. I was reading it in the context of prayer, and my whole frame of reference was different. I was listening to it. I was expectant. "What are you saying to me, God, today?"

And on that particular day what came through to me had little to do with the suddenness of Uzzah's death. The question was: was I myself ready for death if it came that suddenly?

I have read that passage often in a prayerful, listening state of mind, but I don't think that particular question ever arose again. Just then it was important to me. There was a close relationship in my life that was in disrepair, and I would not have liked to have died and left it untended.

I experienced the Bible as all the things it has always been: literature and history, letters and prayers, stories whose origins are lost in the dim and ancient past, and stories of Jesus that in contrast seem just yesterday. But for me the Bible became preeminently a medium through which I could hear God in the present.

As I went about my daily chores, I thought about what happened when I read the Bible. I had begun to realize that not every Christian saw the Bible as I did. For instance, I did not believe that every word of the Bible was factually true, as some Christians do. But neither did I feel the great need felt by others to be sure they have the correct modern translation of each word and the proper understanding of the context. These were important, but not most important, and worrying about them while reading the Bible got in the way of prayer. It was being in touch with the living God that was most important. Perhaps nearest to my way of reading the Bible was that of an older generation of Protestants who didn't stop much to think about factual accuracy, but just read the Bible devotionally, that is, prayerfully.

"What you are doing," said the Professor, "is meditating. Or to put it another way, you are listening to the Spirit. Christ told the disciples that he would send the Spirit and that the Spirit would teach them and make all things plain."

"That's what it feels like," I said. "I mean, I know that a lot of the people of the Bible were so open to God that you can feel their relationship. But something more than that happens when I read the Bible. It's God in them and in the Bible and in me. And the Spirit making the connection."

"Yes," said the Professor, "that's what happens."

7. Saints with a Small s

As both transcendent and immanent God is at once beyond every possible being, yet present and manifest in everyone of these beings.

JOHN MACQUARRIE

Although I still did very little talking about God to anyone other than God or the Professor, I had, when I was baptized, not only become a member of the wider church, but a member of a specific congregation of Christians. I remember that my early feelings about my fellow Christians were that everyone walking through the church door must feel as I did—caught up in wonder and a sense of high adventure. But, of course, they didn't all feel that way and, in time, neither did I. Instead, a deeper and longer lasting perception took place.

Soon after I was baptized, I was asked to edit a publication for the parish. At first I had said no. The idea of producing yet another pink or yellow mimeographed sheet was depressing. And then I suddenly thought, "Why does so much produced by local churches have to look—and be—amateurish? Why not give the very best we can produce to God and the parish?"

And so I said yes and persuaded others to join me. This was the beginning of a Christian community that went on from producing the magazine to running a school for ourselves and others to deepen our understanding of the faith.

How do such communities happen? Although I was the editor of the magazine and the director of the school, it was not my doing, no matter how well or poorly I worked. As Jesus said of the Spirit, "The wind bloweth where it listeth."[1] The wind of the Spirit swept down and touched us, one here, one there, and gathered us together. For the most part, it was a quiet wind, an inner stirring. The Spirit moved within the context of our own lives and our stumbling efforts to find and follow God.

At the first meeting of the board of the magazine, I felt such a stirring. An inner whisper told me that I should open the meeting with a prayer. Now, meetings of laity in our parish did not, to my knowledge, open with a prayer. Prayers were said when clergy were present or they were not said. And although I had lost a bit of my reluctance to be open about God by then, it was still with me, and so the meeting came and went without a prayer.

Afterward, I felt ashamed of my cowardice and determined to do better at the next meeting. When the day came, I put the agenda on a large sheet of newsstock with magic marker and at the top of the list I wrote "Opening Prayer." I could not escape.

I shared my thoughts and feelings with the others, and we discussed it. "Of *course*, we should have a prayer," said one.

"Laity can pray just as well as clergy."

"Better than some," I heard someone mutter.

"Funny, we just leave it to the clergy," said another.

My voice shook a bit, but I prayed a real prayer, a simple one that I had written beforehand.

Was it this discussion that first encouraged people to speak of God in a real way, rather than only speaking of the outer manifestations of the parish activities we were reporting? I don't know, but I do know that the Spirit also touched others in individual ways. Our work began to take on subtle differences from the work of a similar secular committee. For instance, there was the matter of *shepherding*.

Although we wanted parish participation, we also wanted high-quality work and this was not always forthcoming. To edit a parishioner's offering turned out to be a more delicate matter than editing work on a secular magazine. People felt they were giving a bit of their soul to the church and did not like to have their soul edited. We decided that each article and author should have a *shepherd* rather than an editor, someone who could lovingly and, yes, prayerfully bring out the best that the writer could offer.

As we struggled with these and other problems and rejoiced when things went well, our sense of Christian community deepened. More and more often in committee meetings we would find our conversations veering away from the exact business before us as we asked each other about this and that aspect of Christianity.

Conversations overflowed the meetings and we would get together for lunch or dinner. Sometimes when two of us met to discuss something as impersonal as an article about the church organ, we would instead find ourselves sharing our deepest concerns. The growing sense among us that God was indeed present, alive, and caring gave us courage and hope.

It was perhaps a year after the magazine had started that two of our members reported identical experiences. While talking to friends about the magazine, they had each used the words: "But it's not just a *magazine*."

But what was it? A "church within a church" sounded arrogant. Indeed, there were those in the parish who objected to our editing people's articles and thought we *were* arrogant. They suggested to the rector that we have a rotating board. We laughed at the impracticality of the idea but were a bit disturbed by the charge. Even to say "community" was not quite right, as it was never sharply defined. Husbands and wives, friends and supporters, and those we prayed for seemed in some way to belong. We knew also that we were part of the parish and part of the larger church made up of all Christians everywhere. There was even a sense from time to time of being one with all the Christians who had gone before us.

One day when I was visiting the Professor, I told her about this awareness we had of being "not just a magazine."

"Do you remember," she said, "when you told me that you wished that the Protestant Reformers had not thrown out the idea of canonized saints?"

"Yes."

"Well, it wasn't a purely negative action," she replied. "They wanted to reemphasize 'the communion of saints,' the fact that we are *all* saints. That's what the communion of saints means. I think that's what you are sensing."

The words were there in the Apostles' Creed, but I had never thought about them much: "I believe in . . . the communion of saints." I wondered what it had meant to Christians when the creed was formulated, and I looked it up. I found that in the fifth century Bishop Nicetas wrote, "What is the Church but the congregation of all saints?" Those "who have lived, or are now alive, or shall live in time to come, comprise the Church . . . of which Christ is declared the head. . . . In this Church you will attain to the communion of saints."[2]

I don't remember ever using the term to the others as an explanation of what we felt. The word "saints" was too open to misunderstanding. But in my heart, I knew the Professor was right. What we *could* know and acknowledge, at least to ourselves, was that we were simply a handful of people who grew to know that we had been touched, been graced, by something beyond ourselves, and we knew it together.

Every shepherding session had the potential of enlarging our community. I don't mean that we consciously evangelized, but the sense of the present reality of God, alive and involved in people's lives, is marvelously attractive. We didn't need to evangelize. One of us would be talking to a friend about daily happenings or to an author about an article and the subject would begin to shift. "I never have understood the Trinity," someone might say. "I mean, how can God be one and also three? That sounds silly."

"But how else could the disciples explain it?" we would reply. "I mean, there they were, good Jews believing in one God, and then there was Jesus, their companion who died and was resurrected, and they saw and touched him. And before he left them, he told them to wait and pray and the Holy Spirit would come, and the Holy Spirit did come. They didn't sit down and say, 'This must be the Trinity' or write a theology book or anything, but they knew they'd experienced God in three ways."

"Oh. Is *that* all it is?" our questioner would respond.

"Well, not exactly *all*," one of us would say, suddenly conscious of our ignorance, "but it's enough to go on."

"But that happened a long time ago. What do you mean 'to *go* on'?"

And suddenly we would find ourselves in a deeper and more personal place than we had expected. Haltingly, we would try to say something of the God we prayed to, of Christ, our companion in humanity and suffering whose life and death redeemed ours, and of the Spirit, that great inner Teacher.

We felt we did not do these impromptu teachings well, and we became more and more conscious of our ignorance. We also began to sense a restlessness among us. "I wish," one of us said at a staff meeting, "we could share these meetings with more people."

"The people I'm thinking of," said another, "really aren't interested in working on the magazine. They just want to talk about God."

Where did these people come from who wanted to talk about God? We met them in the context of our lives—at committee meetings and dinner parties, on the train and in the supermarket. We never buttonholed them and began talking of God, but we had learned the value of speaking the truth from the heart, and if the subject of God was pertinent or—as was more likely—we could see that the person was reaching toward the subject, we would speak.

With increasing frequency, we found that friends would urge us to talk with someone, often a complete stranger. "But why? What are we supposed to talk about?"

"I think they want to talk about God," our friend would answer. And so a date would be made with a social pretext of lunch or tea, and there we would be, expected to break the ice and talk about God. Although daunting in prospect, in practice this was seldom difficult. There was, we were learning, a tremendous spiritual hunger in many people, and it needed only a friendly word or so to have them share their stories.

Once, for instance, a friend called me and asked, "Do you know A. T.?"

"No," I replied, "but I've heard of her. She has arthritis, doesn't she?"

"Yes, very bad arthritis. She's just gotten out of the hospital, and I think you should see her."

"You mean about God?"

"Yes. Would you?"

"Well, yes. But I don't think I can manage it without an introduction."

"She has a swimming pool. Suppose I ask her if I can bring you swimming some day?"

"Sure. I'll come."

And so it was that a few days later, I found myself in one corner of a heated pool talking about God with a complete stranger while my friend tactfully paddled around at the other end.

"When I was in the hospital," said A., "and could hardly move, I was somehow sure that there was a Bible in the bureau drawer. I don't know how I managed to get out of bed, but I did. There *was* a Bible there, but when I got back in bed, I found that I couldn't read it, my eyes weren't working very well. I strained and strained and finally I read just one sentence. It said, 'I cried unto the Lord in my despair!' Later—something happened—I can't describe it," she said, "but I just sort of said 'Yes, God.'"

"And then," she continued, "I began to improve. I don't mean I'm cured, but I'm well enough to do some living. I want to learn something about God. And prayer."

Some people only wanted one or two conversations, but more and more we found people who, like A., wanted something ongoing. "What are we going to do with all these people?" we asked each other.

Concurrently, we became more and more aware of all that we ourselves wished to learn and slowly the idea of having a school for ourselves and others became clear in our minds. "A School for the Laity," someone said.

"Yes, and taught by laity," said another.

Our rector was blessedly supportive both then and later. "Why not retain the Professor as an advisor?" he suggested.

The Professor was delighted and so were we. "Now move slowly," she said. And so a handful of us left the magazine and spent a trial year in teaching each other and planning the school.

As a human institution the school was unremarkable. There were no sophisticated learning systems. Instead, we had a tough course of thirty lectures in basic Christian knowledge in large part taught by the students themselves. Each student/teacher would read several fat tomes recommended by the Professor and her colleagues at the seminary and sometimes spend as much as a year in preparation for giving one lecture. But we had been very right about the interest. On opening night, over seventy people registered. Over the thirty sessions attendance averaged forty-five, not seventy, but enthusiasm remained high. We had a center now, a place for people to come, a spiritual home. We could learn and teach and grow together.

It was now five years since I had been baptized. I was no longer drunk with my newfound faith. No longer did I see everyone who entered the church door in a pink glow. But when on a Sunday I saw those I knew and had grown to love moving slowly toward the Communion rail, I felt something much deeper and truer. These were no longer strangers in polite Sunday clothes. I knew something of their hearts. I knew their courage, their failures, their confusions, their hopes, their prayers. They carried these with them as they walked toward the altar, ready to give their best and their worst to Christ and have Christ make them his own. Spiritually I went with them as they walked and knelt. And I knew they went with me.

8. The Larger Company

The saint is a saint not because he is good, but because he is transparent for something that is larger than he is.

PAUL TILLICH

I've always loved books. As a child, they were both an escape from fear and hurt and a window to other worlds. By the time the escape became less necessary, the habit of reading was well established. I read biographies, novels, adventure stories, plays, myths, encyclopedia articles, and how-to books. I tried anything, put aside what I didn't like, and read what I liked. But until I met the Professor, few of these books concerned religion. The Professor fed me the right books at the right time, and I began to learn my way around in the field so that I recognized names and subjects and could do an intelligent job of finding books myself.

The Bible and books on prayer and theology were central to my reading, but while browsing in library or bookstore I found books in yet another category: the lives of saints. It was for me a bonanza discovery. I felt like a child given an unexpected treasure chest. The lives of saints were more engrossing than novels.

My understanding of sanctity changed radically as I read. I had previously pictured saints as people with a pious sameness about them who, as they came closer and closer to God, merged into some sort of great white light. Instead, I discovered tremendous variety in them and, as they grew in sanctity, they became even more themselves, more individual. I had also thought of saints as being so impossibly good that we could not understand them. Instead, I found them to be wonderfully human and so utterly without pretense that their humanity was easily visible. I, whose childhood battles had left me overly concerned about what people thought, was greatly moved by the casual attitude of saints toward their own inadequacies and their utter disregard of people's opinions.

Some biographers, of course, have obscured the humanity of their subjects, often burying the lives of early saints in legend. But even legend sometimes allows this lack of pretense and sheer humanity to show through. St. Christopher, for instance, is so legendary that in this century the Catholic church decided to take him off their list of saints. Yet his story has always spoken to me.[1]

Christopher lived in the early days of Christianity and, according to the legend, was martyred in one of the great persecutions of the church. The legend depicts him as a giant of a man with more strength than brains. Very proud of his strength, he decided that he wanted to serve the greatest king in the world and no one else. So off he went in search of the greatest king. After long travels, Christopher believed that he had found him and joyfully entered his service. But when Christopher had served the king for some time, he found that the king was afraid of the devil.

"The devil must be greater," thought Christopher, "and I only want to serve the greatest." So off he went in search of the devil.

After another long search, Christopher found the devil in the guise of a cruel knight and entered into his service. But here again he was disappointed. The devil, it turned out, was afraid of Christ, so our single-minded friend went in search of Christ.

Now Christopher was not a Christian himself, and Christians were hard to find in those days of persecution, but at last he found a holy hermit who told him of Christ.

"How may I serve him?" asked Christopher.

"You must fast," said the hermit.

But Christopher didn't think he'd be very good at fasting and asked for another way. "Well then," said the hermit, "you must pray. Pray during the day and wake at night and pray again."

"I don't understand what prayer is," said Christopher, "and I don't think I'd be any good at that either."

The hermit did not seem to be discouraged and suggested yet another way to serve Christ. "Stand by the river," he said, "and carry people across."

Christopher accepted this task, built a little house by the river, and lived there, carrying all who needed help across the river.

One day, after a long time of faithful service, a child came to him and asked to be carried over. As Christopher strode into the river and began to cross, the child weighed heavier and heavier on his shoulders. When he had staggered to the other bank, Christopher said to the child that he felt as if he were carrying the whole world. And the child replied that he had not only carried the world on his shoulders, but Jesus Christ who had made the world.

I puzzled over why this legend spoke to me. I am not a man and, far from being proud of my strength, I am totally unathletic. And prayer, which meant nothing to Christopher, had by that time come to mean a great deal to me. Yet the story did speak to me. What came through was that Christopher was himself and insisted on being himself. He rejected any suggestion that he be anything else. He would not conform to what he was told was holy, but single-mindedly held to his desire to serve—in his own way—the greatest king in the world.

Sometimes saints have written down something of their own lives or disciples have taken down their words. I found that these words often spoke to me with great freshness and immediacy. Certainly Teresa of Avila's did. Teresa, a nun who lived in sixteenth-century Spain, was a reformer of the Carmelites.[2] Her tremendously active life was based on prayer. She was a contemplative and a mystic. But not at first. For twenty years after her entrance into the convent, she alternately prayed and struggled to pray. "When I was enjoying worldly pleasures," she wrote, "I felt sorrow when I remembered what I owed to God; when I was with God, I grew restless because of worldly affections."[3] And further: "Over a period of several years, I was more occupied in wishing my hour of prayer were over, and in listening for the clock to strike, than in thinking of things that were good."[4] Blessed Teresa!

It was, of course, not only their lack of pretense that spoke to me and sent me again and again to library and bookstore searching for the life of yet another saint, it was their holiness. What do I mean by holiness? Holiness is something that makes you want to fall to your knees, that puts you in awe. Your instinctive reaction to a saint is, "My God, *this* is what a human being can be!" And then you realize, with awful clarity, what you yourself are. Yet at the same time, saints' transparent ordinariness and human struggles give you hope of lessening the gap between you and them by an inch or so.

It was, I realized, their love of God—and God's of them—that gave them the strength to go on. We speak blithely of loving God. It is the first commandment. But for the most part ours is a foggy, ephemeral love. With the saints I found it was tremendously real. When you read Augustine's words, "Lord, thou didst strike my heart with thy Word and I loved thee," you realize that Augustine *loved* God. Those words are not merely a creedal statement. "It is always springtime in the heart that loves God," said John Vianney. It is not so much that the saints love God as it is that they are *in* love with God. And their actions match their words. In their own way they each gave their life to "the greatest king in the world."

It was, above all, this tremendous *wedding* of the human and the holy that spoke to me. At one and the same time they were perfectly ordinary human beings and people in whom God shone through.

Their humanity was underlined by the very diversity of their lives. In the nineteenth century there was John Vianney whose words I just quoted.[5] Most familiarly known as the Curé d'Ars, Vianney was a French priest who had so much difficulty with his studies that he was almost unable to become a priest. Placed in Ars, an extremely poor and unimportant village, his holiness shone so clearly that first the villagers and eventually people from all over France sought him out.

What was I to think, proper Episcopalian that I was, of this shockingly ascetic priest who spent sixteen hours a day in the confessional? It was not my culture, my century, or my denomination, yet there was no doubt in my mind that he was holy.

Then there was Thérèse of Lisieux. Thérèse has been compared unfavorably with the Spanish Teresa. When Ida Goerres, the German biographer, decided to write Thérèse's biography,[6] the author's intellectual friends were astounded. "Why Thérèse of Lisieux?" they asked, the implication being that no intellectuals worth their salt would be interested in such a bourgeois and dull saint. But it was just this dullness that challenged Ida Goerres. It is somehow easier for us to picture a saint as having come either from poor peasant stock or a family of great wealth. For a saint to come from a household of sentimental religiosity seems as if God has bad taste. Nor did Thérèse have long to become a saint—she died at twenty-four. Yet Thérèse indubitably *was* a saint, and her "little way" of small services of love and self-denial became a pattern many thousands have followed.

The lives of saints always exhibit at least some miracles. Among older saints, hagiography takes over, that confusing custom of embellishing a saint's life with scores of miracles, many sounding quite unlikely and others quite unchristian. About sixth-century St. Columba, John McNeill, author of *The Celtic Churches*, observes, "The actual events of Columba's life are obscured behind a cloud of miracles."[7] But with later saints, miracles are carefully and believably documented. The Curé d'Ars often had such detailed knowledge of the lives of strangers coming to him for confession that it can only be described as miraculous. Saint Teresa of Avila sometimes found herself lifted into the air when she was praying. It is hard to *disbelieve* this when she describes in her autobiography how she asked the nuns to hold her down so that visitors would not see her rise from the floor.[8] Such levitation is not common, but miracle healings are very frequently documented, many of them—as in the case of St. Thérèse of Lisieux—occurring after the saint's death.

Although I found myself impatient with hagiography, I did not dismiss all miracles as being improbable or impossible. There were enough so well-documented ones that it seemed ridiculous not to believe them. Some modern scholars go to great lengths to show how miracles can really be explained away scientifically. I can remember reading an article "proving" that Joan of Arc's voices were caused by tuberculosis of the bones. Well, perhaps they were, but surely God can use both our health and our infirmities to communicate with us. "Miracles," said St. Augustine, "are not contrary to nature, but to what we know of nature." What I certainly did believe was that saints had spiritual powers beyond the rest of us. And I also believed that spirit could influence matter.

Anglicans consider themselves both Catholic and Protestant. The Protestant half of me kept asking, "Are there no Protestant saints?"

They wouldn't, of course, have been canonized, but had there never been Protestants as holy as canonized saints? I went searching in libraries and bookstores for Protestant saints and I found them. They might not have satisfied the requirements for canonization, but they had that same all-consuming devotion to God and stubborn obedience to God's will in the face of great difficulties and opposition.

There was, for example, Mary Slessor.[9] Brought up in the slums of Dundee in the late nineteenth century, she went to work in the mills at age eleven. There were seven children in the family, their father was a drunkard, and they lived in one room. The two bright spots in her life were her mother, a devout Presbyterian, and Sunday church, which became an oasis of cleanliness, peace, and learning. Hearing the sermons of missionaries returning from Calabar (now Nigeria), she early determined to go to Calabar as a missionary. She went to night school, got permission to read books beside her loom in the mill, and eventually acquired enough education to be a missionary and was sent to Calabar.

The slave trade—although ended—had left life in Calabar in chaos and horror. Small tribes warred with each other. Witchcraft prevailed. If anything went wrong, "witches" were accused and made to take poison. If they survived, they were innocent, but few survived. Minor misdemeanors were punished by flogging that ended in death. People were sacrificed at funerals. Twins were always killed because they brought bad luck. Missionary efforts were primarily contained in three adjacent towns. To go far from these towns and into the jungle alone was considered certain death. Yet the towns themselves were far from a haven of safety, as over half of the missionaries died of disease.

Mary Slessor spent a great deal of her life arguing. She had argued for her right to go to Calabar and, once there, pled to go into the jungle. In her Bible, crisscrossed with comments, she even took on St. Paul, writing beside one passage, "Nae, Paul Laddie."[10] But she also wrote, "God and one are always a majority."[11] She was sure that God wanted her to go to the tribes in the interior and eventually she received permission to go.

Once in the villages of the interior, she lived as simply as the villagers did (in dirt-floored huts with no protection from mosquitoes or rats) and eventually grew to understand and love these fierce people. But her relationship with them was one of constant arguing, cajoling, and defiance. She stole twin babies and brought them up, put herself in front of people they were going to flog, and sheltered those accused of witchcraft. For almost forty years she labored under incredible conditions, becoming *Eka Kpukpro Owo* (Mother of all Peoples) to countless villages, but always pushing farther into new and dangerous territories.

I read the lives of scores of other saints and holy people: early martyrs in the Roman amphitheaters, learned scholars, people devoted to the poor, and people devoted to prayer. There were classic saints like Augustine and Francis, and there were Protestant Reformers like Luther and Wesley. There was the American Quaker John Woolman,[12] today's Mother Teresa,[13] and yesterday's Dag Hammarskjöld.[14] All of them were tremendously human and very individual, yet all of them were so infused with God that it changed them and many around them.

As saint after saint passed before me, I found it tremendously affirming. Here, perhaps more startlingly than in any other way, I could see God in the world. However close Jesus is to us in spirit, it was a long time ago that he walked the shores of Galilee. The saints are nearer in time, and their lives bear witness to his life and to God's presence in the world.

I have been writing of saints as individuals, yet they are, of course, part of the communion of saints. I think that if I had only read of saints and not found a Christian community, I would still have had some sense of the communion of saints, but it was my Christian friends, those very real people, who brought it home to me. Christ had said, "When two or three are gathered together in my name, I am in the midst of them." It was true. And because of this, I was more easily able to sense our relatedness to all Christians, including the great saints of history. Taken together, we form an immense and timeless body of people to whom Christ was—and is—a present reality.

9. God in Everyday Life

God, in his supreme manifestation, where the fullness of His Being finds its final expression . . . is the Shekinah, the presence and immanence of God in the whole of creation.

GERSHOM G. SCHOLEM

For the first ten years of our marriage, we lived on a dead-end street of twenty small houses. But by the time of the School for the Laity, we and our three children had moved to an old Victorian house and started a new life-style. Into its ample rooms came a succession of people to live with us for a few days, a few months, or sometimes a few years. There was the pregnant and unwed actress waiting for her baby to be born, the young Hungarian refugee, the director of the teenage center who came while looking for an apartment and stayed two years. Because of our connection with India, there were scores of Indians and also a friend from Thailand. There were au pair girls from England, France, and Sweden, followed by a housekeeper from Trinidad. When living arrangements for her four teenage children in Trinidad broke down for the second time, we told her to go and bring them to our house. They became part of our household too and started a steel band who played "Jesu, Joy of Man's Desiring" at our twenty-fifth wedding anniversary. A torrent of life flowed through our home.

The word picture I have drawn depicts a happy life, and it was, but it was not "smiling snapshot" simple. Neither our family nor any I knew in our growing Christian community had an unpressured or pain-free life. We lived in a highly competitive society where expectations for parent and child were great.

When these expectations were not met, pain and conflict followed.

On the face of it, the school and its people only added more work and stress to the lives of everyone involved. But it also sustained us. More and more we saw our community as something of wonder. We were caught up in a great adventure; our lives were shown to us in a different light by God and by each other. Hurts were healed, hope was given. Deep friendships developed. We were blessed, and we knew it. In gratitude we felt a need to be involved with problems outside our own circle. The lives of the poor and hungry, the misery of injustice and oppression, and the horror of war called one of us here and another there to do what we could to change matters.

The books the Professor had given me to read about prayer seemed to be mostly by or about monks and nuns, saints, and hermits, or at least by clergy or academic theologians. It constantly surprised me that what they wrote fitted our lives at all, but somehow we made what we read our own and worked out ways of prayer that fitted our life-styles. Waiting in the car to pick up the children, I would get out my prayer book; lying in bed before sleep, I would talk over the day with the Lord. Hard pressed for privacy, I would lock myself in the bathroom to meditate. Sometimes two or three of us would go for a picnic lunch and have a few minutes of silent or spoken prayer together. I remember a friend's report about getting out her prayer book in an amusement park while the children were on the Bump'em Cars. One man said that the commuter train had become his cloister.

But the fact remained that we were not in a cloister. We were neither saints nor hermits, and although wonderfully supported by clergy, we were not clergy. We were perfectly ordinary laity.

"Why," I asked the Professor, "is so little written about groups like ours? Practically the only people I've read about who get excited about God are individuals, and most of those are saints. We are just ordinary people."

"What you need," she replied, "is a history of the laity. I'll find you one."

She found me one, and I read it with fascination.[1] Today most denominations pay more attention to the ministry of the laity than they did twenty years ago. Then, the division between clergy and laity was so taken for granted that we seldom even thought about it. The book, therefore, did more than give me information; it opened my eyes to the existing situation. We had come to a place where we seemed to think that there were two classes of Christian citizens: the upper class, which consisted of clergy, monks, and nuns, and the lower class, which consisted of all the rest of us. The upper class was supposed to lead and the lower to follow.

Christians, I discovered, had not started out with such a distinct division between priests and laity. In the early church it was believed that baptism "ordained" the Christian into the royal priesthood of the church, and although the difference between clergy and laity was there, it was more a matter of function than degree. The royal priesthood, the priesthood of all believers, was taken seriously by both clergy and lay people. But as the church grew, it increasingly needed order and organization, and the clergy assumed more importance.

At times, I reflected, the clergy have misused and do misuse their authority and power. But as I looked at our parish in comparison with the early church, what came home to me with tremendous force had little to do with the clergy and everything to do with the laity: *Those early Christians knew their faith.* They knew it inside out and upside down. They taught it in city and village, in the famous catechetical school in Alexandria, and argued competently with bishops in synods. And we, although we were improving, were ill-equipped to be part of a royal priesthood.

It was good to know something of the history of the laity, but it did not fully satisfy my inner questioning. I realized that when I had asked the Professor about "groups like ours" what

interested me most was the way we found, served, and worshiped God in the midst of everyday life. We knew that God
was with us, in us, around us, and not just in church.

When my thoughts about God in everyday life finally began
to fall into place, it was through an unexpected means. I was
browsing in a bookstore one day when I found Martin Buber's
books on Hasidism.[2] Today books of Hasidic tales are commonplace and Martin Buber is remembered primarily for his later
book, *I and Thou*, but at the time I had never heard of Hasidism,
and Martin Buber was just a name to me.

It is always interesting to read of a way of life and belief far
distant from your own, and I started reading Buber's books on
Hasidism in this frame of mind. It was like going to a slide
lecture about some country you have never been in and never
intend to go to. I was, therefore, startled when I found Buber's
words touching something deep within me, and I read everything I could find on Hasidism.

Hasidism arose in eighteenth-century Poland. It emphasized
a teaching of Jewish mysticism found in the later Kabbala. In
this teaching sparks of God's divine presence, or *Shekinah*, are
in all creation. In the Kabbala this was an intellectual/mystical
belief, but in Hasidism it was transformed into a way of life that
could be undertaken by the simplest peasant. There was no
person, no object, no action that could not be rendered sacred.
The world was pregnant with holiness and everyone was called
to be midwife. Yet, with all this emphasis on Immanence, the
Hasidism seemed to be simultaneously more conscious of Transcendence rather than less. It was the very opposite of separat-
ing the sacred and the secular, the clergy and the laity, heaven
and earth. It was falling on your knees before God's presence
in the world.

No matter how strange were Hasidic beliefs, no matter that
they were Jewish and not Christian, this wedding of heaven
and earth, this Immanence that was never divorced from Transcendence was my way also—not, of course, in its particulars
of theology or practice, but in its emphasis on God in the world.

It was X in the sassafras leaf, God in me, in the stodgy woman in the elevator, and in my husband and my children. It was God in my friends whether Christian, Jewish, or Hindu. It was God in prophet and psalm and Gospel, and God in the praying reader. It was the Holy Spirit touching and teaching us in our Christian community. It was Christ in sacrament, in "Saint" and "saint."

Before reading about Hasidism, my thinking about Immanence as a doctrine had seldom been deliberate. When I had come across mention of God in the world in the line of a hymn or the words of a theologian, I had simply rejoiced. The doctrine of Immanence, I had presumed, was utterly central to Christianity. Didn't God make the world, come to the world, and redeem the world? But Hasidism, with its whole way of life centered on God *in* the world as well as beyond it, made me reluctantly realize that Immanence was not the emphasis of all Christians. Some Christians emphasize the secular—ethics and good works—in the name of Christianity, but with no seeming consciousness of God's presence in and around them. Others emphasize the sacred. God is to be found in church on Sunday, in sacred writ and ceremony, and that is about all. I exaggerate. But it took exaggeration for me to understand how I had, on the one hand, taken the doctrine of Immanence for granted in the Christian faith and, on the other hand, felt a certain unformulated longing for Immanence to be more openly emphasized, explored, and praised.

"Why," I now asked the Professor, "don't more Christian writers write about Immanence?"

The Professor laughed. "More questions! You really should go to seminary, you know."

"The seminary doesn't take women."[3]

"This one doesn't," she replied, "but the ecumenical seminary does."[4]

"I can't imagine their taking me with only a degree in painting."

"You could ask," said the Professor.

But for the time being, the subject was dropped and we returned to my question. "There are not as many as you might like, but there *are* Christian writers," she said, "with just as Immanent a spirituality as yours. You've even read some of them! When you go home, look on your bookshelves for your friends."

On the way home on the train, I thought about Immanence as expressed in Christian writing. The Bible, I realized, was full of it. In the Psalms God was right there, involved in people's emotions and seen in nature where rivers and hills clapped their hands in joy to the Lord. That reminded me of my favorite canticle. I had my prayer book with me, and I took it out and turned the pages to the *Benedicite Omnia Opera.*[5] It goes on verse after verse like the following:

> Glorify the Lord, every shower of rain and fall of
>   dew, all winds and fire and heat.
> Winter and summer, glorify the Lord,
>   praise him and highly exalt him for ever.
>
> Glorify the Lord, O nights and days,
>   O shining light and enfolding dark.
> Storm clouds and thunderbolts, glorify the Lord,
>   praise him and highly exalt him for ever.

I'd loved it for years before I discovered that it was believed to be a misplaced part of the book of Daniel representing what Shadrach, Mishach and Abednego sang in the fiery furnace where they had been thrown by King Nebuchadnezzar. The *Benedicite* is not just a reflective poem about God and nature; it is an outpouring of love for God, and it is love expressed in and through the world.

Who among Christian writers wrote of God in similar fashion? Riding on the train, I couldn't seem to remember and I couldn't wait to get home and look for books by those friends the Professor had assured me expressed a spirituality of Immanence.

It was the next day, after the children had left for school, before I had time to look for books. I stood in front of my bookshelves and stared at the titles.

"Ah, there was Teilhard de Chardin."

My eyes glanced at his *Phenomenon of Man*, which expresses his scientific thinking, but I did not take it down. What interested me most were his writings on spirituality. I reached for his *Hymn of the Universe*, took it off the shelf, and laid it on my desk. Then I added *The Divine Milieu*, sat down, browsed through the familiar volumes, and thought about Teilhard's spirituality.

To Teilhard, Spirit and matter are inextricably mixed, and the incarnation of Christ affirmed the truth of his view. When he writes about *matter*, Teilhard is not using the word narrowly in a purely scientific sense, but to refer to matter in ordinary human experience. "Matter," he writes in *The Divine Milieu*, "is the assemblage of things, energies and creatures which surround us." In practice, says Teilhard, "matter is not just the weight that drags us down, the mire that sucks us in, the bramble that bars our way. . . . It is simply the slope on which we can go up just as well as go down, the medium that can uphold just as well as give way, the wind that can overthrow or lift up."[6] Teilhard seldom, if ever, uses the word *Immanence*, but he was clearly talking of a spirituality where the emphasis was on finding, following, and worshiping God in the world.

My eyes went back to the bookshelves, and this time they stopped at Thomas Kelly's *Testament of Devotion*. Thomas Kelly was an American Quaker who, for me, epitomized all that is most wonderful about the Friends, that combination of hearing the Holy Spirit and responding in love in some of the darkest areas of life.

I took down the book, flipped it open, and read:

Deep within us all there is an amazing inner sanctuary of the soul, a holy place, a Divine Center, a speaking Voice, to which we may continuously return. Eternity is at our hearts, pressing upon our time-torn lives, warming us with intimations of an astounding destiny, calling us home unto itself. . . . It is a Light Within which illumines the face of God and casts new shadows and new glories upon the face of men. It is a seed stirring to life if we do not choke it. It is the Shekinah of the soul, the Presence in the midst. Here is the Slumbering Christ, stirring to be awakened, to become the soul we clothe in earthly form and action. And He is within us all.[7]

It pleased me that Kelly mentioned the Shekinah.

I took one last book from the shelves, *Prayers* by Michel Quoist. He is a French priest whose remarkable book of prayers was written out of the experience of living and working in the slums of Le Havre. "If only we knew how to look at life as God sees it," writes Abbé Quoist, "we would realize that nothing is secular in the world."[8] He saw God in a telephone call, a wire fence, a lurid poster, the subway. "If we knew how to listen to God, if we knew how to look around us, our whole life would become prayer."[9]

I moved over to my comfortable reading chair and sat down to think. All three of these writers gave me the same sense of God in the world that Hasidism did. There were other books on my shelves with an emphasis on Immanence—not many, but there were a few. But these three writers emphasized the radical combination of the sacred and the secular. Not only were the sacred and the secular not separated, but the secular was seen as holy.

10. Meditating on the Bible

To be saved, we have to be unmasked. We have to face our-
selves as we are and the world as it is. This is why the same
question "Where are you?" runs all through the Bible.

SUZANNE DE DIETRICH

"How is meditation going?" asked the Professor on one of my
visits to the seminary.

"I'm not sure it's *going* at all," I replied. "I don't know what's
wrong lately. I just seem to get stuck, staring at a page in the
Bible."

"I think what you need is a method," said the Professor, "an
exercise to get you started."

She hesitated and then reached for a book from her shelves.
"Try reading this. You may not like it, but I think it might help."

The book was Bede Frost's *The Art of Mental Prayer.*[1] I was
glad the Professor had warned me that I might not like it. When
I look at the book now, I wonder how I ever managed to read
it or to follow its instructions without exasperation. The language is archaic and was utterly strange to me on first reading;
I felt it seemed more suitable to a medieval monastery than to
the world in which I lived. The text was full of phrases like
"make a reverence or gesture of self-abasement" or "kneeling,
standing or prostrate on the ground." To me this language and
pattern of action belonged to some distant land or other religion. But everything else the Professor had suggested had come
alive for me, so perhaps this would too. And the book, no
matter how archaic, was utterly clear about what you should
do. Here was a way, a map, a set of instructions to show me
how to put one foot in front of another.

Actually six sets of instructions, or methods, were presented. They had all been developed in the sixteenth century from much earlier forms. The only one I'd ever heard of was the Ignatian method. Developed by St. Ignatius of Loyola, the Ignatian exercises are still very much in use today. The book also described Carmelite, Oratorian, Franciscan, Liguorian, and Salesian methods. The focal point of all of these exercises was either an incident in the life of Christ remembered by heart or a passage of Scripture. I felt challenged and determined.

"I'll see if I can translate them," I thought, "into my own language and something more suitable for our times." Gathering books, Bible, paper, and pencil together, I picked a time of day when the house was quiet and shut myself in my bedroom. And so I began, day after day, step by step, working my way through all the methods, both reading and practicing as I went.

I soon found that I liked parts of some methods and disliked others. I decided to choose those parts of each method that suited me best and to put together my own method, translating some of the terms into more commonly used words. In the end it was this process of forming my own method that really taught me, and I discovered that underneath all of the strange language and practices lay something tremendously workable.

The Ignatian method of meditation and a number of others are called *exercises*. It is a good term, in that these methods provide practice in allowing the Spirit to lead our thoughts and our imaginations, and I found my Bible reading not only came alive again, but was immeasurably enriched. I learned to *expect* to find layer upon layer of meaning. Meaning, I discovered, was not bottled up in a tight web of words. Indeed, where it made most sense to me it was often freest, flitting from one aspect of a truth to another, constantly stretching my head and heart to comprehend a deeper level of truth than I had yet realized.

As I worked with the various methods, I found that once I got underneath the old language they were extremely practical. And foreign though they had seemed to me at first, they worked. By "worked" I mean that the Bible passage I was meditating on would come alive for me. Take, for instance, the story of blind Bartimaeus, whom Jesus healed on the road from Jericho.[2] After reading the passage (according to the method I had made my own), I was supposed to imagine myself in the scene and play it through. I could be part of the crowd or play Bartimaeus, or Jesus, or all three in turn. The meditation went something like this:

I pictured the scene in my mind. There they were, Jesus and his disciples leaving Jericho, followed by a great multitude. For a while, I was one of that multitude. There was excitement in the air. People tried to walk where they could hear what Jesus was saying, and his friends kept having to tell us to move back a bit and give him room.

Then I decided to be blind Bartimaeus. I was blind and sitting by the roadside. I'd heard people pass by, talking as they walked. I'd heard wheels and the hooves of horses, camels, donkeys. But now, far down the road, I heard the noise of many people coming. What was happening? I called out, "Who is coming? Who is coming? Why so many people?" The noise was getting frightening. Should I try to back away? I called out again, "Who is coming?" And at last someone answered me. "It's Jesus of Nazareth," said an unknown voice.

Jesus! He'd been healing people. Hundreds of people. I felt a surge of hope. Oh! If I could just get to him! I called out, "Jesus, Son of David, have mercy on me!"

But he didn't hear me, and others told me to be quiet. Well, I wouldn't be quiet. I called out to him again, "Jesus!" Oh, if I could just *see!* Where was he? And then something happened. I heard someone talking, but I couldn't hear what was said, and then a man nearer to me called, "Bartimaeus, you're in luck! Get up. He's calling to you."

I got up so quickly that my cloak fell off. Where was he? I put my hands out before me, but I'd forgotten the ditch. I stumbled and fell. Hands pulled me up, I was passed from person to person, and then suddenly it was very quiet and I knew I was there, in front of Jesus.

"What do you want me to do for you?" asked Jesus.

"Master," I said, "give me my sight back."

When it happened, it was very simple. Jesus just said, "Go your way. Your faith has healed you."

And suddenly I could see! There in front of me was Jesus. He smiled at me. He was the first thing I saw. I said, "I will never leave you."

Even though the above is an example of an imaginative replaying of the Bible story, it is often called "the reading." Now I moved into the meditation proper. I was no longer Bartimaeus. I was myself thinking about what I had just read and imagined. At this point in the method I had developed, I had to decide what facets of the story had come home to me most strongly, repeatedly, or had an element of surprise.

One element of the story had startled me. Jesus had called a *blind* man to come to him. It was my realization of how strange this was that made me imagine Bartimaeus falling in the ditch. Why didn't Jesus go to the blind man? Why call him to come, stumbling in the ditch, bumping into people all the way? Another part that came home to me with great force was my imaginative experience of being blind: the reliance on sound, on the help of others, the frustration of trying to lead a full life while reduced by blindness to a half life. And finally I was struck by Bartimaeus's instant decision that his way was to follow the Lord.

The next step was to ask myself what these aspects of the story said about living our lives, about our relations with God and with other people. In thinking of these, I was not supposed to limit my thoughts to what happened on that road near Jericho, but to range widely and consider anything that the story suggested to my mind.

I turned first to why Jesus called the blind man to come to him. What did it mean? Why hadn't Jesus simply walked over to the blind man? It seemed thoughtless, but it must have been the opposite.

We are all blind, of course—blind to many of our faults, blind to what we should do and where we should go, having distorted views of ourselves and others, turning blind eyes to God for fear we will see too much. And then my thoughts followed another vein: If we are physically blind, we must rely on other senses and on other people. Do we do that when we have a blindness of the Spirit? Sometimes. Those whose emotions are hidden behind defenses turn to intellectual pursuits. Those who vaguely know that there is something lacking or immature about their personality try to compensate in other ways.

"Go thy way," said Jesus when he had restored Bartimaeus's sight. But Bartimaeus's *way* had been the way of the blind. He could not go back to it. Yet Jesus did not ask Bartimaeus to follow him. It was Bartimaeus who made the decision.

My mind turned then to what the living God might be saying to me through that story: I could not seem to get away from seeing how much was left up to Bartimaeus. He called to Jesus insistently, even when the crowd told him to be quiet. He responded to Jesus' request that he come stumbling to him in the dark. Jesus even asked Bartimaeus to say what he wanted. And, last, once he was no longer blind, he immediately decided to follow Jesus.

What was left that I was supposed to think about? Did I wait too much for answers, for clarity, for seeing and understanding to just come to me? I was certainly always asking the Professor questions and trying to figure things out—I loved to think and I loved to read—but I disliked studying.

"That's the problem." said God.

"What do you mean?" I asked.

"You keep trying to reinvent the wheel. It's good to think so much, but why do you keep avoiding the hard books? You got a great deal out of the book on meditation when you didn't even like it. You aren't the only one who has done some thinking you know."

I paused a minute. I'd never thought about it, but it was certainly true. "What should I read?" I asked.

"That's up to you," said God.

11. Spiritual Direction

Confide your thoughts to a man who, though he lack learn-ing, has studied the work in practice.

ST. ISAAC THE SYRIAN

It was perhaps inevitable that my closest friend in our School for the Laity would sooner or later ask me for spiritual direction. She saw what I had gained and wanted to grow as I had grown.

"Would you," she said one day, "teach me to pray as the Professor has taught you?"

"You mean *direct* you?" I replied.

"Yes."

"You could ask the Professor."

"No, I want you."

I paused. A whole mixture of thoughts and feelings swept through me.

"This *couldn't* be the way it was supposed to happen. It had only been two years since I started going to the Professor. Besides, she *was* a Professor and what did I know? Very little."

I was not immune to feeling honored. I savored it a moment and then felt shame for having done so. It was God my friend wanted and not me.

I needed the Professor's advice. Surely she would say I wasn't ready and that would be that.

I saw the Professor every two or three months and communicated by letter in between. We seldom phoned each other, but I decided that this question wouldn't wait, so I called her.

"How do you feel?" asked the Professor after I had explained the situation.

"Frightened," I replied. "It isn't just what I don't know. I'm afraid that I'll get in God's way."

"What do you mean?"

There was a long pause. "Pride, I guess. I'm a good teacher and it's a tremendous compliment to be asked to help someone learn to pray. I'm afraid I'll get carried away by my own ideas and tell her what to do or how to act instead of how to listen to God. I'm afraid for her and afraid for myself."

"Now you know," said the Professor softly, "what the fear of God means."

"Yes." I felt a shudder go through me.

"Then it's all right for you to direct her. Just call me if you have problems."

During the years the Professor directed me, I had felt no need to think about the process of directing. But when first one and then another friend from the School asked me to direct them, I found myself thinking long and hard about what they really wanted, what I could teach them, and what spiritual direction was in the Christian tradition.

In a sense, I felt that I already knew what the tradition said about spiritual direction, but I found that I couldn't quite put it in words. What was it that the Professor did for me? She taught me about prayer and theology and the Bible, but there was something behind those that embraced them all.

My mind went back to when I had first gone to the Professor. I'd been out of touch with God and not knowing what to do about it. The Professor showed me ways of prayer that helped me to get back in relationship with God.

A *relationship!* That was the key word, a relationship with God. It was what I had built in those years before I went to the Professor and what she helped me restore. As in a human relationship, I had gotten to know God in conversation, by doing things together, by trying and failing and being forgiven and trying again.

Twenty-five years have gone by since I began directing people, and my thoughts have not changed on this central issue. A relationship with God is the essence of a spiritual life, a life of prayer, mysticism, and the inner commitment of all Christians. It is so basic that it is often overlooked, and people go off on tangents thinking the tangents are the center. Spiritual direction is helping someone to build his or her relationship with God, and it is primarily concerned with prayer.

To most people "prayer" means "prayers," those words said to God in church, in times of need, and more frequently by a devout few. But, as I had learned from the Professor, there is a rich tradition in Christian spirituality of prayer understood as a way of life and of a central and guiding relationship that illumines all other relationships. In retrospect, I realized how fortunate I had been not only to find the Professor, but before that to have been too shy to talk to anyone about God but God. In shyness and ignorance, I had stumbled into that essence of Christian spirituality, a relationship with God.

It was prayer that formed the basis for directing my friend. What kinds of prayer did she pray? When? Regularly? What went on in her heart and mind when she prayed? Perhaps she should try a certain method of prayer, or read a particular book, or read the Bible more, or think about God in a new way. And, of course, I prayed for her and with her. For all my fear of the responsibility, the practice of directing seemed—at least at that point—to be very simple.

I had been directing my friend for about a year when she asked me, "What would it take to persuade you to teach a group of people some of the things that you have been teaching me?"

I was feeling very overcommitted at the time and, after thinking a moment, said, "The assurance that there would be no work."

From this conversation there came into being something we called *Prayer Workshops*. These were small groups in which we would simply discuss various aspects of prayer. In due course, a number of the participants asked me for individual spiritual direction.

The people I directed were not, however, limited to people from the workshops or the School. Friends referred people from other churches or those with no church affiliation. Teenage children of my friends came to ask help on a paper they were writing, stayed to talk of God, wrote to me from college, and came again on vacation. Once a complete stranger called me up and said that she had heard from a friend that I both had an interest in India and was a spiritual director. She was an American Hindu, she said, but had recently left a Hindu convent after a three-year stay and wanted to go back to Christianity. Would I take her on? After several exploratory sessions, I agreed to direct her.

"I don't quite understand how I became a director," I said to the Professor one day. "I certainly didn't plan to be one. It just sort of happened."

"That's the way it works," she replied. "It isn't a matter of taking a degree in direction or being ordained. It's a matter of people coming to ask for help."

Today there are programs in spiritual direction leading to a degree or a certificate. I suppose if these programs had been available when I first began directing, I would have taken one. But somehow I am happier without any official recognition. Yet such a simple path to a difficult ministry demands safeguards. I never, for instance, suggest to people that they might come to me for direction. Sometimes I can see that they want to for a year or two before they come, but even then, I wait for them to speak first. The greatest safeguard lies in the knowledge that I am doing this in the sight of God. If I am somewhat transparent to directees, I am wholly transparent to God. Directing is for God, with God, and to God.

Helping people to build their relationship with God provides the most obviously Immanent experience I know. There are times when I hear someone's shy and halting description of their search for God and know with a deep knowing that God is acting in their lives and is acting at that very moment. Sometimes I have felt such awe that I have had a hard time preventing myself from falling on my knees to worship God in the person in front of me.

Although circumstances, individual needs, and previous knowledge vary, my first sessions with a directee are apt to follow a similar pattern. I will have suggested that we meet several times before we decide that this is the right thing to do. In those sessions I simply want to get to know them a bit. What is their background? Why did they come to me? What did they hope to gain from direction? And then I tell them what they can expect from me. "Direction," I might say, "is concerned with helping someone to build his or her relationship with God. One's relationship with God is mostly based on prayer, so a great deal of what we'll talk about is prayer: what your understanding of prayer is, what kinds of prayer you use, and when you pray. Does this make sense to you, and would you still like me to do it?"

If they say yes, I bring up for discussion and mutual agreement how often we will meet, where, and whether we will write or phone in between meetings. And unless we are already friends I usually ask that we not socialize so that we keep the focus on the relationship with God.

Traditionally, directors are not paid, and I have never accepted payment. Much directing is done by clergy and is considered part of their job, so in a sense they are paid even though no fee is asked. Some clergy and graduates of programs in spiritual direction work independently and do charge fees. I feel fortunate that I have never had to charge.

I mentioned a *rule of prayer* earlier when describing my being directed by the Professor. Most people first coming to direction have a natural rule. They might, for instance, go to church on

Sunday, talk over the day with God when they go to bed, and read the Bible or a spiritual book several hours a week. After discussing these practices, I suggest additions or changes. The directee argues or agrees, and we eventually reach mutual agreement. It is not, at least not in my experience and practice, a matter of your director handing you a rule of prayer and saying, "Do it this way," but of working out, with your director's help, ways of prayer that seem best for you and then committing yourself to try to follow them. Obedience is essentially given to God and to your own resolves rather than to the director.

In my own life and the lives of others, I have found two aspects of rule to be of great importance. The first lies simply in having a rule, as opposed to praying hit or miss in whatever fashion strikes you at the moment. The second is the honest reporting of how well or poorly you have kept your rule. Perhaps you haven't kept your rule at all or the kinds of prayer are not for you. On the other hand, you may have been too scrupulous in keeping it. In all likelihood, one kind of prayer has gone well and another has not. Such discussions are not narrow. The directee's problems in prayer, failures, successes, understandings, and misunderstandings raise many questions. Is the relationship with God an honest one? Does he have a distorted idea of God? Or why does she favor one kind of prayer over another? Sometimes such questions are clearly topics for discussion. At other times, they must be slowly worked out between God and the directee.

Neither in my own experience nor in tradition does direction keep to this simple pattern. But time and again I return to the central question: "How are you praying?" Here, I believe, in honest, humble, searching discussion you are very close to God and to the heart of directing.

In the modern resurgence of interest in spiritual direction, many directors prefer to think of direction as Christian friendship and dislike any title other than *friend*. I prefer to use the term *director* because I am not primarily talking about a relationship between two people, but between one person and God. Nonetheless, friendship is often a natural outgrowth of direction. C. S. Lewis in *The Four Loves* describes friendship as two people who stand side by side and look at the same thing.[1] In this sense friendship is also an active part of direction. What you are both looking at is the relationship of one of you to God. You are companions in this task and often you are also very conscious of being companions with Christ.

One of the reasons why some directors would rather be called "friend" is that they don't want to set themselves up as being wiser or better than the person seeking guidance. Yet no one who gives spiritual direction under any name can help being taken as an example, regardless of whether he or she is a good or bad example. The tendency of many is to idealize their director. Sometimes this is merely exasperating to the director, but at other times it is tremendously humbling. You hear high praise, know that it is meant, and inwardly cringe. You know you are not like that, you are far from that. It is frightening and drives you to your knees. No amount of denying the compliment and saying that you are "just a friend" will change the person's attitude. Indeed, it often makes a directee think more highly of you. In my experience, there is only one way out of this dilemma. For want of a better term, I call it *transparency*. Being transparent means that nothing is hidden. I don't mean by this that you use the directee as a dumping ground for all your problems, but that you put up no front. You take direction seriously, but yourself lightly. One of the best, true compliments I have ever received came to me once when someone reported a conversation between two others. A person who knew me only as a teacher was trying to put me on a pedestal. The other one, whom I directed, replied, "But don't you see? She isn't that good and that's just what's so wonderful!"

One of the more obvious jobs of a director is one-to-one teaching. This varies tremendously from directee to directee, depending on individual needs. One person may seek direction, as I did, knowing nothing of teachings on prayer and very little about Christianity. On the other hand, I once directed a man whose knowledge of theology was vast. What he didn't know was how to pray. It is the latter, "how to pray," that is the most vital knowledge a director has to impart. Here teaching becomes more like *coaching*. The director does not, of course, watch a directee at prayer, but questions about how prayer is going, suggestions for alternate methods, and reminders of what has been forgotten are central.

The knowledge that the director imparts, I believe, should never be parroted from books but, in so far as possible, should be familiar from use. A director doesn't need to be able to pray with the fervor of a saint or reach advanced stages of the spiritual life but should have some inkling of what prayer must be like for a saint. On a lower level, different kinds of prayer should be as familiar as breathing; the Bible should be an old friend and theology make sense in daily living.

The most unique task of a spiritual director is *discernment*. One needs to discern, among other things, what books and what methods of prayer might be helpful to a particular person at a particular time. Each of us is a unique child of God, and a director must have the wisdom, the generosity, and the strength to help people to grow in their own way.

The above is little more than a good tutor would do for a pupil. But discernment gets more demanding. All of us have areas of knowledge or action we wish to avoid or to emphasize, not for sound reasons, but for neurotic ones. Often we are blind to these. We are not only blind, but we have built up strong and elaborate defenses to hide the motivating reasons from ourselves and others. Here the director enters an area where discernment is sometimes tremendously difficult. Is, for instance, a directee's longing for silence and solitude in which to be with God something inspired by God and wonderfully right, or is it—at least in part—a neurotic need to escape from people? It might be either or both.

It would seem to be only common sense in this day and age for the director to have a basic grasp of modern psychotherapy, not for the purpose of doing therapy but for recognizing psychological growth and problems. Related to this, the director should also be able to recognize clearly which personal neuroses might distort his or her own judgment. Yet, in spite of the usefulness of some knowledge of psychology, discernment is not primarily dependent on it—it is dependent on the Holy Spirit, for directing is not only about prayer, it is impossible without prayer. In the last analysis, it depends on the openness of both the director and the person you are directing to the leading of the Spirit. It is not so much a matter of praying for the person you are directing—although that is vital—as it is of letting God use your knowledge, experience, and common sense. Or, to put it more simply, letting God use *you*.

It is strange how we think it only right and proper to ask God's help, but we hesitate to say that God sometimes works through us. Somehow it is considered more modest to take the credit ourselves. But the credit is not ours, and it always comforts me when directees recognize this. Once a directee wrote, "Thank you for letting God use you for the 'dirty work'—for caring enough to be 'straight out' with me. Over and over again now, I hear the answer you gave so swiftly you could not have thought of it. It seemed to be but the medium through which the Word came."

My directing has been at its best when I have known without a shadow of doubt that God has used me. Once one of my directees had just done something of which she was horribly ashamed. She was utterly mired in feelings of despair and sat in my study with her head buried in her hands. No words of mine penetrated, and I didn't know what to do. But God did, and I found myself caught up in a tremendous peace and surety. It was so strong I knew it must be showing on my face, so I told her over and over, "Look at me. Just look at me." Finally, she did, and it was all right, as I knew it would be. Afterward she said to me wonderingly, "You were the love of God to me." And I knew she was right and that the action had been God's, not mine.

12. How to Meditate Without Leaving the World

A heathen once asked Rabbi Joshua ben Karhah, "Why did God speak to Moses from a thornbush?"

Rabbi Joshua replied, "If He had spoken from a carob tree or a sycamore you would have asked me the same question. However, so as not to send you away without an answer I would say, God spoke from the thornbush to teach that there is no place where the Divine Presence is not, even in a lowly thornbush."

MIDRASH

I had come to believe that meditation was central to one's relationship with God. Learning to read the Bible in the context of prayer (which is really a form of meditation) had made a deep and lasting difference in my life. Later this was enriched by working out a method of biblical meditation based on traditional spiritual exercises.[1] These two deliberately prayerful approaches to the Bible opened the door for me to listening to God through all of the happenings of everyday life. I found that God was always whispering—waiting to be heard. Meditation was simply stopping to listen. The more I practiced it, the more easily I could hear those whispers. It was, therefore, natural that I would think it important that the people I was directing should learn to meditate.

But my first attempts to teach meditation ended in failure. I would talk about reading the Bible meditatively or explain my method, step by step, and the directee would seem to understand and be eager to try.

"And how is meditation going?" I would ask a few weeks later (as the Professor had once asked me). Almost invariably it would not be going well. Sitting alone with a Bible and trying to go through the steps of a method of meditation, an individual would often just feel a bit foolish, get easily sidetracked, and give up. In attempting to read the Bible meditatively others found that they wanted to know—in the intellectual sense of the word—everything that could be known about the passage for meditation, and this need got in the way of a simple listening to the message coming to them *through* the passage. In neither case could they simply let go and follow the guidance of the Spirit.

Thinking about this problem one day, I decided that it might be easier to meditate in a small group than alone. I could lead the members through the steps with a few words of instruction and then we could be in silence with the Spirit.

"But should we begin with the Bible?" I asked myself. "If methods of meditation are exercises so that we can learn to hear God not only through the Bible but through everything in the created world, why not use the same method but meditate on objects from nature? Once people have had some practice, we can turn back to the Bible."

And so, we tried it. I still remember the first time we meditated together. There were only three of us, and we met in my study, a book-lined basement room that was once the kitchen of our old Victorian house. I explained what we were going to do, said a prayer, and silently handed each of them a maple leaf.

"Be a child," I said in my quiet instructions. "Take a five-minute vacation and just look at the leaf. Five minutes is a long time and the only thing you have to do is to look at the leaf. Examine it, see how it is formed, enjoy it."

In the meditative exercise, looking at the leaf was the equivalent of reading and imaging a Bible story. From there on, the method we used was much the same as for a biblical meditation, but the mood of the meditators was completely different than when they had tried it on the Bible and alone. To meditate on a leaf didn't seem that important, certainly not as important as the Bible. They could relax, and when they relaxed, they let God in. Not only that, but after several sessions of meditating on natural objects, I found that we could return to meditating on the Bible and do so in an equally open manner. My small classes grew, and soon I was teaching twice a week.

It is now over twenty years since that first class, and I have taught off and on ever since. My method has changed little, but like most teachers, I have learned more from teaching than I ever taught. First of all, I've found that it is of prime importance that the opening prayer be *prayed* by both the leader and the participants. Just that simple offering of God's time back to God and a commitment to listen during that time make a profound difference. This is particularly true when meditating on a natural object, because there is nothing else to keep it from being a creative but completely secular enterprise.

There is a theoretical side as well as a practical side to this turning of the will to God, because it is an acknowledgment of God's immanence in the minds and hearts of the participants, in the Bible, and in the natural object. One may call this—as Teilhard does—"extensions of the Incarnation" or simply refer to "God's presence," but the sense is the same. It is the recognition that God is alive, accessible, and in the world.

"What," asked a participant in a meditation class one day, "is the difference between what we are doing and Eastern meditation?"

In every new group of students this question was always raised. Indeed, I had asked it of myself. I consulted Hindu and Christian friends, wrote to friends in India for books,[2] and studied and thought about the question.

On a practical level I found it easy enough to see the similarities between the many forms of meditation. In all cases, you are asked to concentrate on something—breathing, sitting still, saying a mantra or a Bible verse over and over, or losing your-

self in examining a leaf or a passage of Scripture. By this con-
centration, you clear away the busyness in your mind and enter
a state of being that is at one and the same time unusually
peaceful and unusually aware. But there the similarities between the forms of meditation end, for the underlying beliefs
about the world and God differ.

In Hinduism the dominant belief is that only God exists. The
world—all material things—are *maya*, or illusion. This belief is
called *monism*. But to Christians and Jews, the world (matter)
and God (Spirit) are both very real. This is called *dualism*.

These different beliefs give rise to different spiritual aims.
The monist works toward the full realization that only God exists. The dualist practices living in dialogue with God. Yet one
does not have to look far to find Christians who sound like
Buddhists (Buddhism arose from a Hindu base) or Hindus who
sound like Christians.

Shankara, the great Hindu philosopher of the ninth century,
taught complete monism. He saw ultimate reality as the impersonal world spirit. All else was illusion. Shankara's teaching
remains the most influential among intellectual Hindus to this
day, but other great thinkers modified it. Chief among these
was Ramanjua who, in the tenth century, taught a qualified
monism in which ultimate reality has a personality, and the
human soul is separate enough from this ultimate reality to
leave room for worship. The eleventh to the nineteenth centuries were the golden age of *Bhakti*, or the way of love, in which
many Hindu teachers preached the importance of devotion to
God.

But if Hinduism sometimes tended toward affirming the existence of the world—or at least the existence of the worshiper—Christianity also has its world-denying side. Long ago the
Professor had said I should balance my *via positiva* (being reminded of God by things in the world) with the *via negativa*
(remembering that God is beyond the world), and I grew to
love some expressions of the negative way such as these words

of an anonymous woman of the Beguine sisterhood in the twelfth century:

> In love's pure abandon
> No created good can exist.
> For love strips of all form
> Those whom it receives in its simplicity.
>
> Freed from every modality,
> Alien to every image
> Is the life here below
> Of the poor in spirit.[3]

To love God beyond the world is not, of course, the same thing as saying that nothing exists but God. One cannot have love without both beloved and lover. Yet the emphasis of the *via negativa* is certainly nearer to monism than the kind of meditation that listens to God through a leaf or a passage of the Bible.

Worship seemed to be the bridge (or the dividing line) between monism and dualism. To worship takes two, God and the worshiper. Yet the highest reaches of Christian contemplation are both wordless and imageless. The subtleties of these opposing poles of thought have played hide-and-seek in my mind for many years. Christian contemplative prayer sounds similar to Hindu and Buddhist meditation, and there has been a tendency to equate the two. Yet I do not believe that they are identical. Even if our way of prayer becomes wordless and imageless, Christ is there and, with Christ, the world he loves.

13. Spiritual and Psychological Growth

Whether you like it or not, whether you know it or not, secretly nature seeks, hunts, tries to ferret out the track on which God may be found.

MEISTER ECKHART

There was no doubt in my mind that I had grown psychologically as well as spiritually. Ghosts of my childhood still haunted me (and still do today), but I knew them as ghosts and they impeded me less and less. Now, while directing people, I saw signs of such growth in others.

What did this mean? Was this spiritual growth or psychotherapeutic growth? Most writers at the time put religion and psychiatry in different compartments. If someone was "sick," a priest, pastor, or Christian friend should refer the individual to a professional therapist. But I found this division false. There are, of course, people who are clearly very sick, but to a lesser degree we are all sick. As I tried to help people build relationships with God, and as I grew myself, I came to realize that neurosis is a continuum. We are all more or less neurotic; that is, we all have blind spots where our perceptions are askew. Sometimes these distorted perceptions are not only minor, but even endearing to our friends. "Well, isn't that just like Joe" we say with a chuckle about some typical peculiarity. But sometimes these blind spots are not so minor. They keep people from being truly themselves, from reaching out to others, from daring to love, from accepting failure, from accepting success.

A therapist helps clients by building a trusting relationship with them. A director helps directees by aiding them to build a trusting relationship with God. I was not acting as a therapist, but sometimes God was. And I saw people grow.

Such psychological growth was usually slow and gentle, but not always; sometimes it was sudden and strong. Occasionally under a smooth surface I would sense passions ready to explode. Even if I was not acting as a therapist, I felt that I should know more about how people grew and changed. This need became acute when a number of people came to me who clearly needed psychiatric help. Sometimes I would just be a way station for them to gather courage from God to seek the help they needed. But other times the situation was not so simple. One middle-aged man who came to me had seen, we once figured, about fifty professionals during his life. A manic depressive and an alcoholic, he was now earning his living as a day laborer. The kind of sustained psychotherapy open to some of the more affluent in our town was not open to him. But God *was* open to him, and he was seeking God. Was I to turn him away because I was not a trained therapist? I didn't think so, and in time God brought him to health. But I still felt that I should learn more about psychotherapy.

I had read books in the field of psychology and psychiatry hit or miss, but now I began to read more seriously. I also decided that I would be wise to find a psychiatrist to whom I could turn from time to time for consultation. I found one I liked and trusted and after a number of visits I realized that the most useful thing I could do was to concentrate on myself and attain more self-awareness and awareness of others. It was a wise decision, and I stayed with the doctor for therapy and group therapy for many years. But there remained questions I could neither answer in therapy nor find discussed in books or articles. Twenty years ago most books on psychology and religion ignored the relationship between psychological and spiritual growth.

For several years, the Professor had been urging me to go to seminary. "At least just take *one* course," she pleaded. But I resisted. "I learn better from you or on my own," I said. But now I had questions that I could not answer to my satisfaction either on my own or with the Professor's help.

I talked it over with my best friend from the School for the Laity. "I couldn't possibly keep on running the School and go to seminary," I said.

"I think it's important for you to go."

"But I can't just leave."

"I'll run the School," she said, "and there are plenty of people to help. You should go to seminary."

And so I left the School in the able hands of my friend and prepared to go to seminary.

The seminary where the Professor taught still took no women, although it opened its doors to us several years later. I, therefore, went to another seminary that was ecumenical and renowned for its scholarship.[1] By great good fortune, they had a department of psychiatry and religion, and I signed up for courses there as part of my program. On the other hand, prayer as a field of inquiry hardly seemed to exist at the seminary in the 1960s. Therefore, the issue of how it related to psychotherapy was certainly not as urgent in the milieu of the seminary as it was in my own mind. A room in the seminary basement with a sign on the door that read *Meditation Room* symbolized this to me. To call it a "room" hardly seemed accurate—it was the size of a small walk-in closet. There was an altar with a cross on it and a straight chair immediately in front of the altar. If you wanted privacy, you could just barely close the door without hitting the chair.

The seminary did offer a tutorial on prayer taught by a man who later became a good friend. But since I had in effect, been tutored by the Professor for several years, I decided on another option. The seminary had reciprocal arrangements with my Professor's seminary—which *did* have courses in prayer. In this way, I was able to take courses there even though the school didn't yet officially admit women.

Until I went to seminary, I had not stopped to think how different areas of knowledge were divided off from each other in academia. In contrast I had always been interested in how they related. Even the department of psychiatry and religion offered only one course in psychiatry *and* religion. The rest were in psychiatry. It was obvious that there would be no tailor-made answers to my questions about how the two subjects related.

It is impossible for me now to sort out in my mind and put in orderly sequence the times when various insights and bits of knowledge became integrated into a more or less complete picture for me. Certainly the years in seminary and in therapy were learning ones, although many ideas about the relationship between psychological and spiritual growth began long before and others have made sense to me only recently. But it was in seminary that I read most and thought hardest.

I started with the giants, Freud[2] and Jung.[3] It is a bit simplistic to say that Freud did not believe in God and Jung did, but certainly Freud looked at belief in God negatively and Jung viewed it positively. This has meant that Jung's teachings have held a much larger interest for Christians than Freud's. But with one exception neither Freud nor Jung seemed to provide a fertile field for my search. The exception was that both Freud and Jung saw *transference* as a key factor in therapy. Transference means that as you build a relationship with your therapist, you *transfer* to him or her all sorts of feelings that you once held for the giants of your childhood: mother, father, siblings, and others. Now you replay these feelings—many of them unhappy or unfinished—to a happier or at least to a clearer conclusion.

The first basic thing I realized about the relationship between growth in prayer and growth in psychotherapy was that a director tries to avoid transference while a psychotherapist often seeks it. As a director, I did not want all of the childhood emotions of those who came to me for help to be replayed with me as an object. It was *God* they were supposed to relate to, and God was the most perceptive and gentle of therapists.

It was with the writings of Erik Erikson[4] (1902–) and Harry Stack Sullivan[5] (1892–1949) that I began to discover larger possibilities of relating growth in prayer and growth in psychotherapy. It was Erikson's work I noted first. He mapped stages of psychological development as experienced by all human beings from birth to old age. They were simple ones, like an infant's gaining a sense of basic trust and an adolescent a sense of identity. Every stage of development, said Erikson, had the dual possibility of being happily resolved or unhappily aborted. Here were the sources, he said, of emotional problems in later life. Such observations seemed a breath of fresh air and common sense to me.

It was, however, the work of Harry Stack Sullivan I found most helpful. Sullivan, an American psychiatrist, is little known to the general public, yet has had a vast but quiet influence on American psychiatry. Sullivan developed the *interpersonal* view of psychiatry. Both problems and resolutions lay, said Sullivan, in *relationships*. Even in the process of growing up, he wrote, a person with an injurious relationship at one stage may have the resulting distorted perception at least partially corrected by a good relationship in the next stage. Here was therapy that was not in the therapist's office, but in life.

These broad understandings of human personality helped me to widen my view of therapy. I began to think in terms of *growth* and *regrowth*. One grew, one's image of self and others developed in relationship with mother, father, sibling, friend, teacher, lover. One grew through relationships and one regrew through relationships. The regrowth could occur through a relationship with a friend, with a therapist, with people in a therapy group, or with God.

When the terminology of either prayer or psychotherapy gets technical and mysterious, I take comfort in those simple words "growth" and "regrowth." "Growth" is the realm of developmental psychology. "Regrowth" is the realm of psychotherapy and prayer.

And God? God, I realized, is in all the ways of growth and regrowth. From a purely secular point of view, I could dismiss God's part in this regrowth and say that long before Freud, spiritual directors found psychological techniques that helped troubled people. But if the secular view can be so sweeping, so can the spiritual. An Immanent spirituality constantly reminds us that everything and everyone in life has the potential of carrying a message from God. This includes professional therapists, but does not stop there. As Abbé Quoist says: "If we knew how to listen to God, if we knew how to look around us, our whole life would become prayer."[6] We relate to God not only through the words and silence of our prayers, but through the prayerful perception of life around us. When God thinks we are ready to grow, or when we "stand at the door and knock," the Spirit sends us an experience, words, a human relationship, a line of Scripture that brings a fragment of the unconscious to consciousness and replays it in clarity and love so that it no longer has power over us.

As I read more deeply in the fields of psychotherapy and prayer, I found more and more similarities. Sometimes a description of spiritual growth and a description of psychological growth sound practically identical. Yet to say that the same kinds of psychological growth occur in both psychotherapy and a life of prayer does not mean that a relationship with God is just another form of therapy. You enter into psychotherapy with a desire to feel happier and to relate better to the people and world around you. You leave when these aims have been reached. A relationship with God, on the other hand, is life-long, and when you consciously commit yourself to it, you do not know where God will take you. You might be led to sanctity or martyrdom. You might simply be asked to live where you are, but live differently. In prayer you enter into a relation with the Infinite, and the possibilities are infinite.

14. Knowledge and Action

Where, O Lord, am I? If this is east, then east of what or
whom?. . .
The road, O Lord, I have to know the road.
I need to go and come and go again.
Your garden is a prison—or a tomb—without a road.

B. D. NAPIER

As I look back on my three years in seminary, the strongest
memory I have is simply the sheer assault of knowledge,—not
what I learned, but the vastness of it. I had not known that so
much knowledge, so many facts and theories existed. It was as
if I had previously only known water as something contained
in a glass and now found myself in an ocean. I did not feel
ready. Although I had a degree, it was in painting. I had never
lived in a world where scholarship was the norm, while this
particular seminary had a long history of being the academic
home of eminent scholars in all fields of religious knowledge.
Now some of them were my teachers.

Fortunately, I had read omnivorously and, through the Professor's guidance, I had some familiarity with Christian scholarship, but what I had covered now seemed lost in that ocean
of knowledge surrounding me. I had come to find answers, but
I found that there were *many* answers, and I had to understand
and choose between them. Could I "make it" in this world of
scholarship? I didn't know, but I soon found myself caught up
in the excitement of learning.

I had planned my studies with great care so that I was taking
a minimal load in order to have a better chance of keeping up

without neglecting my family. Then a student I had met the previous summer urged me to come and listen to just one lecture in a course on science and religion. It wouldn't, I thought, hurt to just listen for an hour. But it was my undoing.

The teacher, whom I shall refer to as the Doctor, was a genius. I do not just mean that he was unusually intelligent—he had a mind so far above the norm he seemed like a different species. His speciality was physics, but his scholarship was vast and varied. One moment we would be discussing Kierkegaard and the next *Huckleberry Finn*, or the philosophy of mathematics, or the history of the labor movement, or the neurological function of the brain as it acquires knowledge. It was the latter (rather than physics) that was at the center of the course and embraced all other subjects.

Understanding was made easier by the Doctor's humility, tinged, I felt, by loneliness. I'd never stopped to think before how lonely it must be to be a genius. He was tremendously excited by his ideas and needed people to share them with, and we became the recipients of his thoughts. In his humility he had great respect for each and every student.

Every course, I found, needed a different pair of spectacles. Each subject probed deeply in one direction and seldom put on the glasses of any other discipline of knowledge. Yet I found my greatest satisfaction in recognizing or trying to see the relationship of the subjects to each other and to the everyday world from which I had come. It was, for instance, exciting for me to find some theologians referring to the fundamental part that prayer played in the doing of theology. It was not, they thought, just a matter of rational thinking in full control of the scholar, but of the light given by the Holy Spirit. Further counterbalancing the rational side of theology were courses in prayer at the Professor's seminary. Here the relationship of prayer and theology was taken for granted and the relationship of both to the living of our lives encouraged.

I read widely in theology, the works of church fathers like Ireneaus and Origen alternating with those of modern thinkers like Dietrich Bonhoeffer, Karl Barth, Edward Schillebeeckx, John Macquarrie, and John Baillie. I studied Paul Tillich's *Systematic Theology*[1] in depth. I took a long excursion into Eastern Orthodox spirituality. And what I and others read we discussed endlessly in seminars and over coffee cups.

As with all learning, some insights stand out and remain with you. It was from a course in the Old Testament that I gleaned a thought that is still pivotal in my thinking. One of the many readings we were assigned was a book of essays on the Bible by a variety of scholars.[2] In one essay the writer emphasized the importance of being able to differentiate in the Bible between what was factual and what was myth. The word *myth* was obviously used here to indicate something that was *not true*. But in a second essay in the same book, another writer used the word *myth* in an entirely different way. Here myth was seen as a story or image that was a carrier of an important *truth*.

In many ways, these two conflicting understandings of the meaning of myth became symbolic for me of the age in which we live and the books that I was studying. Ever since the Renaissance, theological and biblical studies, like most secular branches of scholarship, seemed to be caught up in an ever-increasing love affair with rationality and provable facts. But now? Were we at a crossroads? Indeed, had we passed the crossroads without knowing it? The doctor seemed to think so. "It is not theology that is dead," he said. "It is science."

Theology, I realized, had in a sense always been agnostic. God is infinite and we are finite. Complete knowledge is impossible. Now it was science that was agnostic. The complete answers to the questions of science were no longer just around the corner; they were perpetually around the corner.

And what of Jesus? Did not God's sending his only Son reveal to us what God was like? Yes, but by faith, not by provable fact. Yet facts play their part, some supporting faith and some challenging it.

"Who was this Jesus who revealed God's nature to us?" The theologians differed. The biblical scholars challenged each other on what little they could say for sure about Jesus. The seminarians wrestled with their personal questions and their own faith, often finding answers in unexpected places. I, for one, certainly didn't expect to find a meaningful answer in studying the early heresies, but I did.

Today *heresy* is almost a popular word. If you write a book billed as heretical, it is sure to sell. But in the early church, heresies were simply discards. They were beliefs about Christ and Christianity that were argued over vehemently in the great church councils before it was decided that they did not describe Christ as most believers knew him.

"Whom," said Jesus to Peter, "do you say that I am?"

And Peter replied, "You are the Christ, the Son of the living God." [3]

But questions remained. It was not until the Council of Nicaea in 325 that Christian beliefs were spelled out as we know them today; they were further detailed at Chalcedon in 451. What were they arguing about? Most of the early heresies were attacking, in one way or another, the Incarnation, the belief that Jesus was really God and really human.

The Docetists, for instance, didn't believe that Jesus really suffered. He only "appeared" to suffer. They couldn't see how *Almighty God* could die an agonizing death as a criminal. "Perhaps," they said, "Judas—or perhaps Simon of Cyrene—had been substituted for Jesus just before the crucifixion."

But if the Docetists didn't want to see Jesus Christ as fully human, the Arians took the opposite tack and denied the *divinity* of Jesus. Christ, they believed, was a kind of intermediate, semidivine being, and God was completely transcendent.

Gnosticism, a complex spiritual movement that was not exclusively Christian but had Christians adherents, went the other way again. Gnostics didn't like the idea of God being or becoming *human* and espoused a purely spiritual religion.

The creeds as we know them today were written in answer to these attempts to deny the coming together of God and man in Christ Jesus. And whatever was left in dispute about Chris-

tianity after those great councils, the Incarnation was affirmed
and reaffirmed. "God of God," says the Nicene Creed, "Light
of Light . . . And was made man."[4]

The whole Christian religion is based on the Incarnation.
Neither redemption nor resurrection make sense without it. But
what excited me was the affirmation that Spirit and matter belong together. If God is not solely Transcendent, we should not
worship solely a Transcendent God. If God came to earth as a
human being, we should not turn our backs on the earth to
seek God. On the contrary, in Jesus, God was a human being,
a human being beset as we are with all the joy and pain of life
and its demands and confusions. How could God have said it
more plainly?

I went to seminary in the late 1960s, that time of tumult over
the Vietnam war and the rise of the counterculture. The tumult
was magnified for me both at the seminary and at home. Coming into the seminary each morning, I would find my off-cam-
pus mailbox filled to overflowing with pleas to come to
meetings against the war and for the poor. Earnest handfuls of
students conferred in the corridors about plans of action. Draft
cards were burned, petitions signed, vehement meetings held
and demonstrations became a way of life. None of this was
more dramatic than in the universities, but the fact that we
were supposedly more than usually devoted to God and
the good heightened awareness. In particular, we were conscious of the fact that the seminary was adjacent to an inner-city
ghetto.

"What was the church doing," I heard repeated in many ways
in student conversations, "ministering to the middle class in
the suburbs? If Christians were truly Christian, they would be
ministering to the poor or be in prison as conscientious objec-
tors."

This question got carried over into classes, and I became un-
comfortably conscious that I was a middle-aged housewife from
the affluent suburbs. Essentially, I agreed with the students. I'd

been supporting efforts toward peace for all of my adult life. And, yes, Christians, myself included, *should* live less luxuriously and spend more time and money in serving the poor. But I thought back to life at home in the suburbs, of my family, my church, and my Christian friends and saw no easy answer. We couldn't just shut down the suburbs and all go somewhere else.

One day in class a student was castigating suburban clergy and I decided to question his position. "Do you mean," I asked, "that every Sunday, suburban clergy should throw verbal brickbats at their congregations from their pulpits and that if they don't, they are not Christian?"

There was a silence for a long moment.

"Yes," he replied, "that's exactly what I think."

Both of us were upset and challenged by this exchange, and each went to talk to a favorite teacher to try to sort it out. It is not an easy matter to sort out.

Jesus was very radical in his demands of his followers. My classmate was right. It is impossible for me to read the Gospels and come up with a picture of "gentle Jesus, meek and mild." To follow Jesus asks for a total self-giving and that—at least on the surface—seems to bear little relationship to comfortable suburban churches.

"Follow me," said Jesus. "Don't stop to bury your father. Let the dead bury the dead."[5]

And to the rich young man who had kept the law from his youth and wanted to know what to do now, he said, "Give all that you have to the poor and come and follow me."[6] And the rich young man went away sorrowfully for he had many possessions.

Was I the rich young man? By the world's standards, we were very Christian. We gave away as much money as we lived on. We worked hard for a better world, we were generous with our home and with friend and neighbor. Yet this was not radical; we lived a very comfortable life.

In the early church, Christians gave all that they had to the church and lived a communal life—like later monks and nuns.

This extreme faded, and few people have seriously suggested that the whole church return to that way of life. But the challenge is there, and every once in a while someone picks it up and reminds us of the radical call of Christianity. In the twelfth century it was St. Francis. He renounced the affluent life he had been enjoying and embraced voluntary poverty. By the time of his death, there were many thousands of Franciscans, Poor Clares (the women's order), and members of the third order (people living in the world, but bound to his principles). Today it is Mother Teresa, serving the poorest of the poor in the slums of Calcutta, who brings us up short and doesn't allow us to settle unchallenged into an undemanding Christianity.

Theologians as well as saints have addressed the radical call of Jesus. Søren Kierkegaard[7] in nineteenth-century Denmark, like my classmate in the twentieth century, severely criticized complacent, middle-class Christianity. He felt that people had lost the sense of being spiritual creatures and believed that each and every Christian should have a personal and radical commitment to Christ.

A voice nearer our own time was that of Dietrich Bonhoeffer, who was executed by the Nazis during World War II. Safe, at the very seminary in which I now found myself, he chose to go back to danger and suffering with his Christian comrades in Germany. God, said Bonhoeffer, should be at the center, not the periphery, of life. Religious activities, he felt, had become the luxury of certain classes. He criticized a view of Christianity that saw it as a comfortable blessing, something "religious" and not involved in the most central and secular concerns. For me, two words of Bonhoeffer summed up my thoughts about being Christian in a suffering world. We should not, said Bonhoeffer, expect God to provide "cheap grace." Grace is God's free gift, but our response should be costly.[8]

What does all this mean for ordinary Christians living comfortable or relatively comfortable lives? Each of us has to answer the question in our own way. I have found many answers in my life. Some have been relatively easy—even joyous. Others have been difficult, and all have been demanding of time, money, energy, or all three. At this writing, I still live and live very comfortably in the suburbs. It bothers me. On the other hand, I do not think Christ asks us to vacate the suburbs. Christianity is not just for saints. It is for all the people who try to be saints and fail. It is for everyone. But I have no doubt that Christ asks us to be unusually aware of suffering and injustice and to work to alleviate them. That we do not do enough is no excuse for doing nothing.

I remember one example: When Martin Luther King, Jr., was shot, many people realized that they had been "doing nothing" about race relations, and I was among them. For Northern Christians the man who had symbolized a Christian way out of a vast injustice was now dead. No longer could we feel comfortably proud of his Christian nonviolence while being removed by geography from the worst of the problem. His death shocked us into an awareness of Northern injustice. Here we were in a white enclave in the North, doing little or nothing to even consider the needs of people in nearby ghettos or to uncover and root out our own prejudice. What could we do?

I phoned the rector and found that he was feeling exactly as I was and asking the same questions. Almost simultaneously we said, "Whatever we do, it must be personal, not distant."

Out of this conversation came a project of getting to know blacks and our own prejudice and of personal involvement with the needs of the poor.[9] The project has grown tremendously over the years, and it has proved to be wonderfully useful. I have not been involved in this endeavor since the early days, but I know many who are. I also know many who befriend the dying, teach the illiterate, or work for peace. It does not make us saints, nor does it redeem us. Only Christ can do that. It is merely "a cup of water" offered in Christ's name, but as an icon points to the God beyond, so such work points beyond ourselves to the suffering of the world. It changes our perspectives on our own life-style, invades our prayers, and influences our votes.

As we try to live our ordinary lives, earn our livings, raise our children, be friends to our friends, be good citizens of our country, and say our prayers, the very thought of trying to do our part in alleviating the suffering of the world overwhelms us. Nor does it help that twentieth-century communications present us daily with yet more needs: Our mail overflows with pleas for the hungry, the deprived, the rejected; the media make such pleas graphic; phone calls besiege us for help. Faced with all the horror and suffering, I have always been comforted by the approach of the Quakers. The words they use to describe one's particular good work are *a concern.* One has a special concern for the blind, or the ill, or the refugee. As Thomas Kelly says, "We cannot die on *every* cross, nor are we expected to."[10]

Your concern is not a good work you get involved in because your friend asks you to, or because it is easy for you, or because it is hard for you and you feel guilty if you don't. It is something that the Holy Spirit calls you to have a *concern* for. Some people find themselves called to one concern all their lives, and it becomes their Christian vocation. They may have unrelated and demanding jobs. They may love their jobs or hate them, but their concern remains. When they read newspapers and magazines, their eyes pick out related subjects. Charitable giving to their concern becomes as automatic as paying the electric bill. In their spare time, they become deeply involved. Other people find that their concerns are several or that they change over the years. In the sense of works of charity, my own concerns have changed many times, yet there has always been an overriding constant that is best expressed as "finding God in the world." It is, of course, not only a matter of finding, but of serving and worshiping God in the world.

I remember once, years before I went to seminary, when this came home to me with startling clarity. For several years I had been spending a day a week with an invalid doing chores and errands for her. She had a disease that played an erratic course, but she had a lively mind and a tremendous will to live. Sometimes she felt well enough to go out in the car and we would go on expeditions, but other times she spent all day in bed. On this particular day she was very sick and didn't even have the energy to think up ways I could help. I thought for a moment. "I know that the visiting nurse isn't coming today," I said. "I was a Nurse's Aide during World War II, and I know how to give a bed bath. Would you like me to give you a bath and change your sheets?"

She said that would be nice and I got ready. It was one thing to see her lying in bed, dressed in soft nightgowns and frilly bed jackets and talking vivaciously about politics or literature. It was another to gently undress her and see a wasted form lying before me, so lacking in energy that I had to help her turn over. Suddenly, I realized that this was not just my invalid friend, this was Christ I was serving.

Christ in the world is not always as obvious as in my invalid friend, nor is Immanence solely concerned with God in people. During my seminary years, my life at home provided intellectual exercise concerning another aspect of God in the world.

After classes I would get on the train and almost immediately fall asleep. It was just as well that I slept on the train because at home I often found myself involved in further deep discussion. My husband was studying for his doctorate in sociology, all three children were in college, and most of the people we saw during those years were nearer our children's age than ours. This immersion in student life, together with our long interest in peace, made it natural for our home to become both forum and refuge for students and dropouts who were searching for answers that made sense. We weren't sure we had answers, but we were willing to talk, and talk we did. Our house resounded to long discussions of war and peace, establishment and counterculture, idealism and practicality.

Our young friends were often more religious than their parents, but they chose various offshoots of Eastern spiritualities that espoused pure spirit. Yet, at the same time, they were passionately concerned with things of this world—peace, justice, and ecology. "Isn't that contradictory?" I asked. "It's Judaism and Christianity that are concerned with both Spirit *and* matter."

But either I was unready to explain this, or they were unready to hear. I did, however, think about it.

The counterculture quoted Suzuki, a Japanese Buddhist, as saying that the ecological problem should be blamed on Judaism and Christianity because the Bible said that God gave man *dominion* over the earth. Well, there may have been times in Christian history when this biblical idea of our dominion has given us the excuse to do ecological harm to the earth and our fellow creatures, but I doubt if we've needed—or used—this excuse. We've acted from ignorance, greed, or necessity—as have many Buddhists, Hindus, and assorted believers and nonbelievers all over the world. Only two things tend to stop us: increasing (and recent) knowledge of how we may ruin our health and food supply and our love of nature.

Love of nature seems to be in large measure instinctive, but it is an instinct supported by the Bible and later Christian writers. In the biblical story as each element of creation was made— land and sea, sun and moon, birds and beasts—"God saw that it was good." The story of creation as told in the Bible is clearly a love story.

This theme of love of the earth and its creatures is repeated here and there in the Psalms and other parts of the Bible. It is not a major theme, but it is strong enough to be picked up by later Christians. The most famous example is St. Francis's *Canticle of the Sun*, which praises the Lord "for Brother Son," "for Sister Moon and for the stars" and for "Mother Earth, who sustains and governs us and brings forth various fruits and bright flowers and green grass."

One of my favorite examples is Gerard Manley Hopkins's "Pied Beauty":

Glory be to God for dappled things—
For skies of couple-colour as a brindled cow;

For rose-moles all in stipple upon trout that swim;
Fresh-firecoal chestnut-falls; finches' wings;
Landscape plotted and pieced—fold, fallow, and plough;
And all trades, their gear and tackle and trim.

All things counter, original, spare, strange;
Whatever is fickle, freckled (who knows how?)
With swift, slow; sweet, sour; adazzle, dim;
He fathers-forth whose beauty is past change:
                                        Praise Him.[11]

Suzuki and Buddhists in general (like Hindus) emphasize the nondualist world and the path of detachment. But, in the usual sense of the word, I am *attached* to nature. Sometimes I am, no doubt, too attached, but it is not detachment that makes me recycle papers, glass, cans, and vegetable peels, it is love of God's creation and of God in creation.

Toward the end of my third year in seminary, I began to feel restless. Perhaps it was the cumulative effect of all the discussions, or perhaps that time of study had just come to a natural end. My original questions about the relationship between growth in prayer and growth in therapy had been answered to my satisfaction: It was all of a piece. Growth and regrowth were of God, whether through prayer, or therapy, or just through living. An Immanent spirituality made sense of this and much more. I had also gained in seminary a more complete sense of self. Self-knowledge and academic knowledge, prayer and theology, intelligence and feelings had become more nearly integrated. I was aware of how little I knew and yet, I realized, I did not want to stay. I had never had any feeling of vocation to the priesthood.

Nor did I want to become an academic theologian. I was more interested in theology for living, in spirituality. And, most strongly, I felt a vocation for being in the world.

But what was I to do? The School for the Laity in my home parish had gone on for a few years after I left and then come to a natural end. "That is the way of the Spirit," said the rector. "It mysteriously sets a fire that blazes for a while and then it is time for it to die down."

Certainly, I felt no desire to try to bring the School to life again. I wanted to write, I decided, but I didn't want to isolate myself from people and I needed a second activity. I went to see one of my professors to talk about it.

"I'd love to teach prayer," I said, "but I'd really like to do it in a seminary. And, of course, that's absurd with my only degree an undergraduate one in painting!"

She paused a moment and said, "I'm not sure. It *would* seem unlikely. But let me make some inquiries for you."

And so a few days later I found myself, totally unexpectedly, sitting in the office of a Roman Catholic priest, a professor in a small Jesuit seminary.[12]

I felt lighthearted. The possibility of anything coming of our meeting seemed as distant as a trip to Tibet, so I didn't need to think too seriously about the results of it and settled down to enjoy our conversation. My host was director of novices and knew spirituality tremendously well.

At the end of about an hour of discussion, the priest paused and then said, "I think I can clear it with the dean for you to teach a two-credit course in spiritual direction to the novices."

I was completely taken aback. It seemed an inconceivable offer.

I waved my hand at his bookcase and said, "But I haven't read all those."

"Oh, I think you have," he said and smiled.

But I hadn't. I'd read some of them, but I felt suddenly overwhelmed by all I didn't know. This was too big a leap for me. I wasn't ready either academically or psychologically. I would have to do something else.

15. Seeking an Immanent Spirituality

If we define God out of this world, we have little reason to wonder that so few are aware of his presence, and so must be counted as irreligious.

CLYDE A. HOLBROOK

As I tried to picture the future pattern of my life after seminary, I realized two things. First, I could not sustain my best writing for more than a few hours a day and, second, I liked to work with people. And so, with more instinct than reason, I decided to start a small publishing company specializing in spirituality.[1]

I knew little of publishing, but I had lived and breathed books since childhood, and I was full of innocent optimism. I had a friend who wrote well, knew what hard work was, had considerable experience in advertising and promotion, and knew how to pray. She said she would be delighted to work with me three days a week on the project.

"Where shall we start?" my friend asked on our first day.

"I think we should start with a few minutes of silent prayer," I replied. We did so every time we met from then on, and I have continued the practice with other co-workers in later years.

Prayer undoubtedly influenced, but did not answer, the question underlying my friend's words: How were we to run a publishing company when we knew nothing about publishing?

"We're going to have to learn what publishing is," I said, "before we do anything."

"How are we going to learn?"

"I can't think how to do it except by reading books and asking people. Can you?"

"No."

And so we began. It was an adventure of discovery. How were books designed? Printed? Bound? Sold?

We read encyclopedia articles. We found the magazines and reference books of the publishing world and studied them inside out. We realized that we had friends who were publishers, printers, paper salesmen, bookstore owners, and accountants. Even complete strangers were willing to talk to us and teach us, and after several months the world of book publishing had become clearer.

"We need two other part-time people," I said one day.

"Someone who can receive the orders, fill them, and keep track of our accounts," replied my colleague.

I laughed, "Yes. But way before that we need a designer and production consultant. My art school training isn't enough to do the job. It's just enough to know that we need an expert."

And so two more colleagues entered our lives. We felt almost ready to begin, but there were still major obstacles. Our production consultant, who had retired after a prestigious career in publishing, warned us of one: "Even very good books," he said, "will never get out of the warehouse if you don't have a distribution system. How are you going to sell these books?"

We didn't know. Most books are sold to bookstores by sales representatives, but we were planning to start with only two books, and no sales representatives we contacted wanted to take on just two books.

"We will have to sell them by mail," said my friend. "We'll just do such a good job that it will work."

There was nothing to do but try.

The other obstacle was related. How could we ask authors to trust us with their manuscripts if we didn't know for sure whether our books would sell? We couldn't. I had not been planning to write for our own company, but we realized that it was the only way to begin. I had been writing several hours a day in between our learning and planning sessions and also working with an artist on a book of words and pictures. Writing, for me, became all of a piece with publishing as I worked with artist and production consultant and talked about advertising and promotion plans. "What's an easy number of pages to make into a book?" I asked our production consultant.

"The easiest," he replied, "are books in multiples of thirty-two."

And so, there I was, counting prospective printed pages before I'd even written a word.

There was a sense of Christian community among us similar to the one I'd experienced in the School for the Laity. God had brought us together and the Spirit was within and between us. There was also a sense that God was in some way within the physical materials we worked with: the paper, the binding, the art work, the design.

We not only lived and worked with a consciousness of an Immanent God but wanted to publish books expressing an Immanent spirituality. I had never found enough books reflecting this emphasis to satisfy me, and it was much harder to find manuscripts. And then one day I happened to read John Macquarrie's *Paths in Spirituality.* It was like finding a spring of water in a desert to encounter a theologian of stature who hoped that in "the restless questing which we see today" we would find an Immanent spirituality. "I doubt," he wrote, "whether the quest can be fulfilled unless we can realize again the presence of a transcendent Reality that is none the less that which is nearest of all, immanent in the world and in human life itself."[2]

As an example of what he meant, he turned to Celtic spirituality. At its very center, he observed, "was an intense sense of presence. The Celt was very much a God-intoxicated man. . . . But this presence was always mediated through some finite this-worldly reality."

The first chance I got after reading Macquarrie's book I went into the city to my seminary library to see what I could find out about Celtic Christianity. After looking in the files, I requested volume 1 of *Carmina Gaedelica*,[3] which contained Celtic prayers collected by Alexander Carmichael in the "Highlands and Islands of Scotland" at the turn of the century. The librarian literally blew the dust off the fat volume before handing it to me. It didn't look as if anyone had opened the book since it was first published in 1900. I still remember my feeling of excitement as I sat down with the book at a desk. And it was a well-justified feeling.

Most of the prayers in *Carmina Gaedelica* were collected by Carmichael in the Outer Hebrides off the western coast of Scotland. They were known by heart in Gaelic by fishermen and crofters, and Carmichael had translated them into a strong, clear English. The prayers reflected the lives of Christians who sensed God's presence in, around, and with them—intertwined with every aspect of their lives. I sat there in the library turning page after page, overcome with the realization that here was a truly Christian spirituality that was just as Immanent in a Christian way as Hasidism was in a Jewish way. One prayer will suffice to illustrate this:

> God to enfold me,
> God to surround me,
> God in my speaking,
> God in my thinking.
>
> God in my sleeping,
> God in my waking,
> God in my watching,
> God in my hoping.
>
> God in my life,
> God in my lips,
> God in my soul,
> God in my heart.
>
> God in my sufficing,
> God in my slumber,

God in mine ever-living soul,
God in mine eternity.[4]

I had an almost instant determination to both publish a se-
lection from Alexander Carmichael's anthology and to learn
more about Celtic spirituality. In the self-paced schedule of our
small press, I was able to do both.

"I'm reading a history of the Outer Hebrides,"[5] I said one day
to my colleague over lunch around the kitchen table. "Do you
know that the Vikings raided the Outer Hebrides *one hundred
years* before anywhere else?"

My friend laughed, "No, I didn't know. How long before that
had Christianity reached them?"

"Well," I mused, "if Patrick came to Ireland in the fifth century and Columba from Ireland to Iona in the Inner Hebrides
in the sixth century, it was probably the seventh century before
the monks from Iona reached the Outer Hebrides. In any case,
the islanders only had something like seventy-five years to practice Christianity before the Vikings came and not only raided,
but made a headquarters in the Outer Hebrides. Things didn't
improve either. The islands became political footballs with a
series of cruel rulers. Later there were feuds between the clans
and then religious turmoil. The spirit of those Immanent prayers we've been reading came through *thirteen centuries* of terrible
conflict and oppression."

"But they sound so peaceful!" said my friend.

"Any peace they had was inner," I replied, "because it certainly wasn't peaceful around them."

"We could do with peace like that today," said my friend.

Although our budget and access to manuscripts were limited,
we also had freedom. If we could find it or create it, we could
publish it. One idea came to us very suddenly and unexpectedly: We should write a vegetarian cookbook for those who
usually eat meat but would like to be, as it were, part-time
vegetarians for reasons of conscience. (It takes eight times as

much grain to produce beef as it takes to produce vegetarian protein, and the world is hungry.) In four months from the conception of the idea, we had written *and* published *Cooking with Conscience*,[6] which in 1988 (some twelve years later) is still in print.

My cottage industry publishing years were not many, but they were joyous, learning, formative years. Our books sold surprisingly well. I became more confident that what I wanted to write and what I liked of others' writing would be of help to readers. Sometimes I was wrong, but we succeeded often enough to encourage us to continue. Unfortunately, something else discouraged us. To make ends meet, we realized we should publish six books a year. But publishing six books would either mean I had to stop writing and concentrate on publishing or hire someone full-time, and I didn't want to do either. The cottage industry was outgrowing the cottage. Reluctantly, we offered to sell our company to the Canterbury Press,[7] a prestigious religious publishing firm in the city, and they accepted.

After we sold our company, I made arrangements to teach prayer at my Professor's old seminary, but there was still work for us to finish. Our last and most ambitious project was a Bible reference book.[8] The very idea of this was daunting, but I said, "Look, we'll just take it step by step the way we have everything else."

After a while we reached the stage of having amassed ten thousand entries on index cards, and they needed to be put in alphabetical order.

"What in the world do we do now?" asked my colleagues.

"We get twenty-six shoe boxes and some helpers," I replied.

So there we were, walking around the dining room table, tossing index cards into twenty-six shoe boxes when the phone rang in the kitchen. Holding a handful of cards, I picked up the phone.

"I'm chairman of the board of the Canterbury Press," he said. "Would you be interested in being its new publisher?"

My mind reeled. The Canterbury Press published sixty books a year while we published four a year at the most.

"Well," he said, "what do you think?"

"It sounds crazy," I blurted out. "Ours is a tiny company. I've never even *worked* in a large company."

"Nonetheless," he asked, "will you think about it?"

"Yes," I replied, "I'll think about it." And I turned and went back to the dining room, still clutching my handful of index cards.

My husband was as incredulous as I, but very supportive. "If they really want you, and you really want to take the job, I think you should do it." But he also warned me how tremendously time-consuming and stressful it was to be a business executive.

Several weeks of interviews and a good deal of thinking and praying followed. I remember most the thought that if I went into such a demanding job, I would have to give up my own writing and once again I would *not* be teaching prayer. Yet the opportunity was a tremendous one. I had been struggling both to acquire and to write a few books to match my dreams. At Canterbury I would have tremendously expanded opportunities. It seemed to be the chance of a lifetime. But could I do the job? I decided that I should leave that to the judgment of the board of directors. Wisely, they had decided to interview seven other people, and it seemed doubtful that I would be the final choice. But, in the end, I was, and I accepted the position.

Fortunately, I was not to be president, and this relieved me of responsibility for a great deal of overall planning and financial and legal matters. It did not, however, relieve me of all of them, and I soon found that my husband had been right about the demanding and stressful nature of the job. From the start, the company was in a marginal financial situation and embroiled in unexpected legal tangles. And while the opportunity to find and publish books was vastly greater than in my own company, we could not afford to pay authors large advances and we were in competition with other publishing houses to acquire the best manuscripts. We would have to work harder and think more creatively if we were to succeed. We could not just wait for manuscripts to come in; we had to think and act. What books would we like to see written? Who could best write them? And how could we persuade them to write for us?

The only way that we could compete with larger companies for the best manuscripts was by persuading authors that we would work with them more closely and take greater care in the editing, designing, and marketing of their books. Often this approach worked. Authors, faced with the mysterious world of publishing where initial query letters may go unanswered for months, where manuscripts take more months to be considered, and where, once the contract is signed, the work of years is out of their hands and vulnerable to the buffetings of business, need someone to trust. This person is their editor. Many of our manuscripts were acquired because our editors—and we had very good ones—seemed (and were) trustworthy to authors.

In my cottage industry days I had experienced God's presence in an ideal work situation. Now I was working long hours under constant pressure, interrupted by frequent crises. Knowing that an avalanche of activity would descend on me at nine o'clock, I would leave home at six and by seven-thirty I was seated at my desk, ready to deal with its daunting pile of papers. An hour later for the few moments before people and problems descended, my assistant would close the door and he and I would have a few moments of silent prayer. Those precious minutes and a few others like them were practically all the time I had for prayer between Sunday and Sunday. Gone were my carefully cultivated daily periods of prayer, meditation, and spiritual reading. I was now in the world of competitive business, and during those pressured years I gained a tremendous respect for those Christians who spend their entire working lives under similar circumstances. Most of them do not even have the reminders of God that I had all around me because of the nature of my work.

Am I saying then that my Immanent spirituality failed me when I became part of a modern American business? No, it did not, because I brought it with me. Of course, to a certain extent I was running on spiritual energies that I had gained in the past when there was more time for prayer. Certainly if I had not had many previous years of finding God in Bible, church, sacrament, and daily prayer, as well as in the midst of life, I would not often have found God in the marketplace. As it was, I had a foundation to build on. An Immanent spirituality is ideal for a busy and pressured life because every person, activity, and object may be a reminder of God's presence. If the Celt could pray over lighting the morning fire and plowing the field, we can pray over phone calls, meetings, interviews, and long, exacting tasks. I don't mean that I always succeeded either in remembering or following God. I failed only too often. But my bias toward seeking God in the world offered me a viable path when time was severely limited.

In another sense I found God everywhere. This was, after all, my business. Both authors and editors were concerned with deep questions about God and the living of our lives. I remember conversations over long publishing lunches, which were far from the fashionable expense-account meals one might imagine. I'd found a modest restaurant—all we could afford—and the simplicity of the place receded into the background as an author and I talked our way ever more deeply into the questions his or her manuscript was trying to answer. I was often conscious of the Spirit's presence in the author, in me, and between us.

No aspect of religious publishing gets very far from basic questions about God. How do we find God? Pray to God? Worship God? What does God want us to do? Sometimes these are asked and answered in a very intellectual way and sometimes in a very simple one, but it always made me think. My mind was stretched as never before, and in a sense I learned more than I ever did in seminary.

16. Darkness and Light

If I say, "Surely the darkness will cover me, and the light around me turn to night," darkness is not dark to you, O Lord; the night is as bright as the day; darkness and light to you are both alike.

PSALM 139:10–11

Jesus said, "I am the light of the world; whoever follows me will not walk in darkness, but will have the light of life."

JOHN 8:12

I did not find God until I was thirty-one years old. As I write these words, I am sixty-four and during most of the intervening years my relations with God, with family, and with friends have constantly gained in understanding and happiness. In the same manner, the opportunities for creativity and satisfying work in my vocation as a Christian writer, teacher, and editor kept expanding. There were, of course, periods of relative sadness or struggle. The ghosts of childhood deprivations still rose from time to time from the depths of my being and distorted my vision, momentarily engulfing me in fears or feelings of rejection, but both prayer and therapy had taught me to see these distortions for the ghosts that they were and to battle them accordingly.

There were other sorrows and failures, the kind that enter everyone's life in the process of living, but none was overwhelming. As my life expanded, I looked at the lives of other people I knew, both rich and poor, who had to deal with profound sorrow and lifelong suffering and I felt that my life was unfairly happy, easy, and fulfilled.

My husband was eight years older than I, but he was a vigorous, active man who seldom even caught a cold. Neither of us, therefore, were much alarmed when he complained of feeling tired. But it continued and got worse.

"You really should get checked out by the doctor, you know," I said.

"I know," he said, rather irritably, "but not today. I've too much to do."

But there soon came a day when there was no question that he was ill, and he let me drive him to the doctor.

"His blood count is dangerously low," said the doctor. "I want you to drive him to the emergency room at the hospital and I'll be right there."

My husband was quiet now, no longer fending off the knowledge that he was ill, but lying very still on the table in the emergency room cubicle. The doctor came, and after a while he sent me into the hall. I watched the nurses and doctors hurrying back and forth and the patients' families waiting—as I was waiting. Time seemed to stand still.

The curtains parted and the doctor came out and motioned me down the corridor. "We can't be sure yet," he said, "but it looks like leukemia. In any case, I'm afraid it is serious."

For three weeks I left my job at lunchtime and went to the hospital to be with my husband. After the first round of blood transfusions, he rallied, but it did not last.

"Sometimes," said the consultant, "older people who have leukemia live for many years. Unfortunately in your husband's case the disease has taken an acute form."

Each afternoon and evening I sat by his bed. For the most part he slept. Sometimes he was in pain.

And then, suddenly, he was dead. It had only been three weeks.

At first shock and the loving support of friends carried me. I wanted the best possible funeral, the most suitable prayers, the best music. No eulogy. He wouldn't have liked one. Our children and I planned the details.

I did not cry, even when two members of the steel band who had learned to play together at our house played "Jesu, Joy of Man's Desiring" at the funeral, just as they had played it at our twenty-fifth wedding anniversary. A friend, whose husband had also died suddenly, said, "You may not feel any grief for months and months. It's too sudden. My friends came up to me and threw their arms around me weeping buckets, and I was dry as a bone."

My experience was the same.

Not feeling grief did not mean just not grieving, but not having any of my normal feelings available to me. I was in a prolonged state of protective shock.

I used to think that certainly within a year after being widowed everything would be shipshape; you would know exactly what you were doing and be long past grieving and making necessary changes in your life. But this was not true for me and I don't think it is true for most widows. Almost three years of my widowhood were a period of darkness and confusion.

Life did not wait for me to recover. Every morning at six o'clock I left the house for my job. Weekends and evenings I faced the piles of letters, papers, and decisions that every widow faces.

I was grateful to be busy and particularly grateful for my job. Everyone on our publishing team was helping us to acquire better and better books. Authors and bookstores were gaining confidence in us.

Widowhood does not occur in a vacuum. A series of happenings now changed my life still more.

My husband had been president of a well-known organization dedicated to working for peace.[1] The founder of this organization now gave $100,000 in my husband's memory. "It is to be for a whole new project," he said, "and I want you to be in charge."

I worked on the project (producing a resource guide of peace materials)[2] in what tiny bits of spare time were available to me. I got exhausted and the project began to crumble before it started. I also had hardly begun to deal with all of the financial, legal, and circumstantial changes that I should consider now that my husband was no longer with me. I still wanted to work, but perhaps I could do a lesser job. The books were planned ahead, and I would be leaving my job as publisher in as good order as possible. The idea of working at home as a half-time editor specializing in books on spirituality seemed a good one. I proposed this idea, it was accepted, and I gave three months' notice.

In publishing you have to plan years ahead. The fall that my husband died we'd enthusiastically described the next spring's list of books to our salespeople, knowing that the following fall would be even better and that the spring a year and a half away would yield many of the kind of books we had been dreaming of. Unfortunately, the Canterbury Press was still in a shaky financial state and a month after I left time ran out, a necessary loan was not granted, and the press was put up for sale.

A publishing company is people-centered. Editors work intimately with authors, with each other, and with other members of the firm. When a publishing company is slated for sale, books, authors, editors, and all concerned are apt to be flung into chaos. They were. Books halfway through the press were stopped and abandoned. The editors and other employees were fired.

My mind reeled and my heart ached. The only comfort I could find in the situation was that good publishing companies vied with each other to buy the press and that most, if not all, of the abandoned manuscripts eventually found fine new publishers.

It was now a year after my husband's death. One day a week I worked on the peace project, doggedly trying to straighten things out. Aside from that day, I seemed to be dealing mostly with the past. There were mountains of personal business and the tail ends of publishing dreams—bewildered authors from the press to comfort and manuscripts to be rescued. I wanted to get on with building my new life, but this also involved looking back.

My husband and I were very different personalities. Our marriage was not made in heaven. We made our marriage by hard work. But over the years, in a way I did not fully realize until after he died, two had become one—one in our style of living, in our decisions, in the way people thought of us, in the way we thought of each other. We remained very different, but our lives dovetailed and were glued together.

Death broke this oneness, but it did not undo my mind-set or rearrange the practicalities of living. For thirty-six years I had been working to make two one. Now this had to be undone.

Where was God in all this?

I tried to pray. I needed prayer. During my publishing years, I had had little time for prayer—although it was somehow bound into the work. Now I had plenty of time and I found prayer almost impossible. My feelings were still numbed, including my feelings about God. God was just an intellectual concept. And reading week after week on the peace project about the probabilities of nuclear war on top of the death of my husband and the death of people's dreams at the press meant that any time I turned inward, I faced a wall of darkness that threatened to engulf me. I would call on God to help me hold it back, but I found myself alone. It was in this state of mind that I was trying to make decisions.

Who was I? What was I to do? What part of the two who had become one should I keep as a present reality rather than just a memory? There was the house. For all of our lives in that made-over but essentially Victorian house, we had welcomed people to share it. There had been the Trinidadian young people, two of whom had played at the funeral, and their mother.

Just recently there had been a young man from Holland involved in the peace movement. My mind went back to the sixties when for several months there was a converted school bus in the driveway. It had a woodburning stove, a stereo system, and five young people who slept there but showered, shaved, ate, and did laundry with us.

This was all part of the two who had become one. This was our life. But was it mine?

While I was still working in New York, my Trinidadian friend had come back to help fill the emptiness and care for the house. Now I no longer needed her and I was alone.

"Avery," I said to myself, "you are selfish. You don't need this big house. A large young family should have it. Besides, your own family responsibilities are at an end" (not that they ever are, but this was the drift of my thoughts). "The children would be agreeable to whatever you choose to do. You could go and live in a small apartment and throw yourself completely into some sort of sacrificial work for the Lord." (I did not have working for Mother Teresa in mind, but that was the general idea.)

When circumstances—job, husband, children—prevent your doing anything really sacrificial, you can always comfort yourself with thoughts about how you might serve God in some great way if only circumstances were different. Well, truth caught up with me. Not only did I not *want* to sacrifice myself in this way, I could not even face moving to an apartment or even a smaller house. I did not have the strength.

Was that just because it was too much undoing too soon, because I was selfish, or because that part of our life together should continue to be mine?

A bit of all three, I think. In any case, I said to myself, "Well, if you can't be saintly, Avery, you can at least be decent and sensible. You need people to help with the chores and to break the haunting silence of the house. It can't be the way it used to be, but you need company, and people need places to stay."

And so I decided to take in housesharers. It was one of the most sensible decisions I've ever made. New life came into the house. Darkness and confusion were held somewhat at bay.

Aside from where I should live, the other big decision was what I should do. As I think is common with many widows and many retirees, I got involved in too many things in trying to fill the unfillable gap and then had to work my way out of most of them. None of these activities, however, provided a central focus, and I needed one.

I had thought earlier of going back to writing, but it posed a problem in that my books had been about prayer. How could I write about prayer when I couldn't pray? Prayer now seemed more possible—sometimes—but great darkness still hovered, and I seldom sensed God's presence.

While still at the press I had met and become friends with an Episcopal monk. Now he was just about to be made the prior of a small priory in South Carolina.[3] A handful of monks lived there in hermitages. My friend was supposed to persuade them to open up the privacy of their lives and share its routines of work and prayer with others. He did persuade them, and I went down for a week's stay. I have gone to the priory twice a year ever since. I found that I could pray there. If *I* did not have the strength to give my life to God in some extreme way, here were people who did. I gathered strength while there and brought it home. Prayer became more possible.

Once I could pray again—even though falteringly—I decided that perhaps I could try writing. As I sat with paper and pencil at the kitchen table early every morning, I realized that I felt closer to God when writing than when praying. The prior said it probably *was* prayer. "Pray the way you are able," he said, "not the way you are unable."

Increasingly, as I stared out the window while deciding what to write next, I found myself open to that very darkness that I had been trying to fend off. Thoughts of death, of annihilation, of the suffering of so many, of the broken images of our culture, of meaninglessness flooded in. And now I did not resist them. For all of those months I had asked God's help to hold back the darkness. When I finally let the darkness envelop me, I found that God was there.

Of course! Why had I ever thought that prayer would be all sweetness and light? Had I believed that God was calmly enjoying choirs of angels in celestial light while pain a thousand times worse than mine engulfed starving children and tortured prisoners? No, God was in the pain.

My writing was not about dark things, but I wrote while conscious of dark things. I was and am always aware of the tension between a simple faith and a complicated secular world.

"I will write," I decided, "about old ways of faith and new ways, about finding God in the world."

Divine Immanence is such a vast and controversial subject that few theologians wish to write about it. Perhaps, I thought, it is too big for theologians; it needs a humbler and more human approach. And so, without forgetting the intellectual questions, I began to write about those times and circumstances in my life when the presence of God in the world has sustained, taught, and challenged me.

This prayerful wrestling with truth slowly brought me back to life. Once I had *accepted* the darkness, a sense of ridiculous adventure began to surface in my life. I was nobody. What was I *doing*, trying to write on vast theological subjects? And working for peace? Would my little bit make one iota of difference in holding back the ultimate darkness we all face? I did not know. But I did know that in my own life, meaninglessness gave way to laughter, to a sense of adventure, to a sense of comradeship with others, to a sense of comradeship with God, to a reborn delight in life. When I had looked for God in the light, God was not there. When I faced the unfaceable, I found that I had joined God in the darkness. And so, paradoxically, the darkness had become light.

17. With All Your Mind

The proper balance of the scales is upset when one ceases to look at the centre; if one gazes at God one is blinded, if one gazes at man one is deafened.

RAIMUNDO PANIKKAR

It was gratitude for a lifetime of finding God in the world that drove me to my writing table early every morning. But as my spirit came out of the darkness and I began to come alive again, my writing became many things for me. It was a review of my life at a time when I needed to review my life, and it was a demanding exercise in the art of writing. It was a recounting of simple personal stories of finding God in the world and of my efforts to connect my experience with theology and Christian tradition. Above all, my writing was prayer. Many theologians have written that doing theology is prayer, and now I knew this truth in my own being.

If I had not felt that I should consider theological issues as well as spiritual ones, my job would have been simpler. But all of my life has reflected an alternation between personal and intellectual considerations, between heart and head. And now the very act of writing caused me to rethink, to think more deeply, and to question what it meant to say that God was present in the universe and to wonder why Immanence seemed to be either controversial or neglected. The more I wrote, the more urgent these questions seemed. "Surely," I told myself, "I shouldn't write without a basic intellectual grasp of what I am writing about. . . ." And so I began to study.

Over the years I had collected books and articles on Immanence. I could not find many, so I had also jotted down the names of other titles and authors that looked promising. I turned to these now and began to read and reread.

For a long time the more I read, the more confused I became. Even definitions did not seem to be in agreement. Louis Bouyer, the distinguished French writer on spirituality, wrote that the ambiguity in the use of the word *immanence* helps to explain "the existence of many interminable theological controversies."[1] What were these ambiguities and controversies? And was it all a matter of misunderstanding or were there real differences?

I knew that some of the confusion lay in the close relationship between theology and philosophy. Both theologians and philosophers employ the word *immanence* to refer to God's presence within us and within everything in the universe. But after that they tend to part company, because when philosophers use the word, they usually mean to imply that God remains within the human mind while theologians mean that God is within (immanent) *as well as* beyond.

It would be a simple matter to use one definition when discussing theology and the other when discussing philosophy if the two subjects were further apart, but theologians and philosophers keep crossing the lines into each other's territory. When a philosophy explains the universe, theologians either want to see how Christianity fits into the picture or to dispute the conclusions, whereas philosophers often want to include considerations of God in their philosophies.

The more deeply I became involved in my writing, the more time I felt that I should give to study and the less time I had to give. I had begun to teach meditation and prayer again, and because there were too many people for one class a week, I taught two. I also still went into the city once a week to work for peace. And then there were people. I had implemented my decision to share my house, and there were always between two and four more or less permanent housesharers. But coincidentally, as my focus on study began to increase, so did the number of people in my house. A friend who lived alone broke her leg on one side and her foot on the other, and I gave her refuge.

One housesharer's eight-year-old son came on vacation, as did my grandson who lived with me when not in college, and the Indian mother and child I mentioned earlier were with us for several weeks.

It was a good life, and I loved it. But I found it hard to study. "I need," I wrote to the Professor, "to shut myself up in a library for a month, where no one can find me."

It was Sunday. I'd been to early church; we'd all had breakfast, and I'd helped bathe the baby. There were a few moments of quiet, and I sat down with the Sunday paper. My eye flicked over the articles in the travel section: "A Traveler's Taste of Vintage France." I didn't want to go to France. I didn't particularly want to go anywhere except to a library. And then, just as I was about to put the travel section aside, my eye caught a heading, "Resident Library in North Wales,"[2] and I began to read.

Yes, you could *stay* in the library. A photograph showed a large room with a cathedral ceiling and walls, alcoves, and galleries of books. Under the photo was a caption: "Theological Reading Room." My lifelong love of books flooded over me, and I immediately imagined myself sitting at one of the reading tables.

The next day I wrote to the library to see if I could qualify as a resident reader. I did, and several months later I was truly there, happily ensconced in an alcove on the gallery with pads of paper and sharpened pencils, facing those very walls of books I had seen in the photograph. My room was just up the stairs and around the corner, meals were served, and I had nothing to distract me from study.

But where was I to begin? The word *immanence* was not even in the card file, presumably because it was too broad a concept. I rummaged in Greek philosophy, studied writings of the church fathers, and delved into the seventeenth-century Jewish philosopher Spinoza[3] (everyone seemed to mention Spinoza). I went back in time to Meister Eckhart,[4] the thirteenth-century German mystic and preacher, and forward again to Nicholas of Cusa,[5] the fifteenth-century cardinal and philosopher. The confusion of centuries, cultures, and beliefs was almost over-whelming. I found no text to guide me, no handy outline. Reading the work of one thinker led me to another, and that one to yet another.

There was one constant: Practically anytime anyone in Western culture has written or spoken about the presence of God in the world in a theological or philosophical sense, they have been subjected to tremendous criticism. Meister Eckhart was tried for heresy. The work of the Modernists,[6] a group of nine-teenth-century Roman Catholic theologians, was condemned in a papal encyclical in 1907. Teilhard de Chardin, a twentieth-century Jesuit, was forbidden permission to publish his books.[7] They only appeared after his death in 1955. Even Nicholas of Cusa, a respected cardinal who was close to the pope, was accused of pantheism, although the charge was quickly dismissed. Of all those who have been so criticized, however, no one was more severely castigated or more influential than Benedict de Spinoza, the Jewish philosopher. He was thrown out of his synagogue, and sentiment against him was so strong that it prevented the publication of his major work, Ethics, until after his death. Spinoza's thinking was subjected to a torrent of passionate invective. Various critics called him "the most celebrated Patron of Atheism in our time," "a monstrosity . . . a wicked and ridiculous chimera," "that incarnate Satan," and "a poisonous spider."[8]

As Spinoza's modern translator Edwin Curley has pointed out, the charges of atheism are ironic when Ethics "begins by arguing at length for God's existence and ends with the conclusion that the knowledge and love of God are man's greatest good."[9]

What was it that Spinoza proclaimed—or seemed to proclaim—that was so shocking? His fundamental idea was that of the "unity of all reality" as the "cause or ground of all that is."[10] This one reality, he said, was God.

Spinoza's thinking seemed to imply the identification of God and nature (the world, matter) as one eternal divine "substance." Now to say that God and the world are identical is pantheism, and Spinoza is commonly referred to today as a pantheist. Tillich disagreed and said that Spinoza did not believe that God *is* everything, but that God is *in* everything.[11]

For over one hundred years, Spinoza's work was subjected to almost universal criticism, but in 1780, this began to change. In July of that year, Gotthold Lessing, a highly revered German philosopher, was nearing his death. His younger colleague Friedrich Jacobi came to see him, and the ensuing conversation so stunned Jacobi that he later wrote it down. What had stunned him was that Lessing confessed to being completely converted to the thought of the despised Spinoza. After Lessing's death, this conversation was made public, and others who had been secret admirers of Spinoza also declared their allegiance. Friedrich Schleiermacher, the Protestant theologian, "even wrote a hymn to St. Spinoza."[13] The tide had turned, and high praise of Spinoza's thought became as commonplace as the insults and criticisms had been in the preceding years.

In the nineteenth century interest in both Immanence and Transcendence among philosophers and theologians was intense because they had the dual and conflicting inheritance of Spinoza's thought and that of Immanuel Kant (1724–1804). Kant's philosophy was the exact opposite of Spinoza's, for he saw God as completely transcendent and beyond our reach.

I had looked forward to reading the works of nineteenth-century thinkers. But as I began to read, I felt let down. By and large, they didn't seem to be asking the same questions I was asking, and from time to time I found myself wondering whether they were really writing about God at all. Both Spinoza and Nicholas of Cusa had used mathematical models, yet I never forgot that they were concerned with God. There was a grandeur about their approach that I missed in many nineteenth-century thinkers.

Friedrich Schleiermacher has been considered the father of modern Protestant theology. Others augmented his work and some took divergent paths, but it was Schleiermacher who gave the nineteenth century its most influential theology,[13] and it was

he who was at the center of the efforts to bring together understandings of Kant's distant God and Spinoza's present God.

One of Schleiermacher's central concepts was that of religion
as "a feeling of absolute dependence." As often as I've read
those words, I still trip over them. Tillich said that Schleiermacher's use of the word *feeling* was an unfortunate choice and
that he really meant an intuition or awareness of the universe,
"of the ground of everything within us."[14] That makes it clearer,
but the statement still seemed to be an answer to a question I
wasn't asking. The fact that there were wellsprings of religious
intuition, or spiritual feeling, within us and that they revealed
the presence of God within and beyond was something I had
first sensed at age ten. Perhaps that wasn't exactly what
Schleiermacher meant, but it was certainly closely related. For
the people of Schleiermacher's time, it was a much needed answer, but for me it was a given.

The nineteenth century was also the time of the Modernist
controversy in the Roman Catholic church. The Modernists
were a group of Catholic theologians and scholars who, to
put it simply, wanted to modernize Catholic thinking.
Some of them had a tendency to espouse such an extreme
Immanence that it seemed to make God a captive of the world
and subject to the capricious intuitions of individuals. This
was very alarming to the leadership of the church, and they
reacted strongly. Pope Leo XIII in an encyclical of 1879 espoused a return to the philosophy of Thomas Aquinas.[15] By the
end of his twenty-five year reign, it had become firmly en-
trenched and even seminary texts had been rewritten.[16] An encyclical of 1907 "repudiated any experiential, affective or
intuitive mode of thought."[17] Intuition was promoted to the upper reaches of prayer with the conclusion that it didn't *belong* to
the realms of theology.[18]

The influence of this monolithic interpretation helped to explain why so few modern Catholics wrote about Immanence.
Not until Vatican II did Catholic doors again open to considerations of Immanence.[19]

I had identified and read something of approximately a dozen other thinkers I felt I should read more thoroughly. Practically all of them wrote a dense and involved prose that often left me studying the same page for an hour, and when I finally understood it, I usually didn't like it. My simple thoughts and feelings were obscured by mountains of theories, few of which seemed to relate to each other, and while reading them I found that I couldn't even remember why I had come to the library.

I closed my books and stared unseeing at the shelves in my alcove. I would, I thought, go out for a walk.

It was spring and the path across the fields was muddy, but the grass was green and it was lambing time. I watched the lambs nuzzling their mothers or bleating in distress because they had wandered too far. I breathed the spring air and relaxed. Loose thoughts floated around in my mind, perching here and there like migrating birds. But migrating birds form themselves into a pattern. Where was the pattern here?

I turned to walk back to the library. Of all the people I had read, I thought, I liked Nicholas of Cusa best. He believed in "the coincidence of opposites."[20] In everything finite, he thought, the infinite is present. God is in everything and everything is in God.[21] I liked that. It was biblical, it was clear, and it said what I believed. But reading Nicholas of Cusa reminded me again of the question of why this coming together of Spirit and matter, which seemed to me so central to the Christian faith, is more often ignored than not, because Nicholas himself was ignored. Aside from a short-lived charge of heresy, no one either called him names or unduly praised him. He was just more or less forgotten until the twentieth century.[22]

Lying in bed the next morning, cuddled under the down comforter and delaying throwing it off to the damp spring air, I thought more about Nicholas of Cusa. Here was a man in the fifteenth century who thought and wrote clearly and profoundly and then, to all intents and purposes, dropped out of history for four centuries. Why? And suddenly I remembered Bonaventure, that saintly and scholarly Franciscan who had lived two centuries earlier. What was it I had been reading about him just the other day? The book was in my room.

I threw back the comforter, put on my robe, went down the hall to make a cup of tea, and came back to settle comfortably in my chair with Ewert Cousin's translation of Bonaventure. And there it was: *"He flourished during the brief period [in the thirteenth century] when spirituality and speculation were not yet separated."*[23]

What happened to separate "spirituality and speculation" was the rise of the great universities in the twelfth and thirteenth centuries. Bonaventure himself studied and taught in one, the University of Paris, but theology and spirituality had not yet become separate disciplines of study as they soon became and have largely remained to this day.

It was still early in the morning, but the library was open and I was thoroughly awake. I dressed and went down the creaky corridor as quietly as I could. What I wanted to read was more about the separation of theology and spirituality. I found it in volume 2 of *The History of Christian Spirituality.*

At the beginning of the fourteenth century a chasm opened irrevocably. The theologian became a specialist in an autonomous field of knowledge, which he could enter by the use of a technique independent of the witness of his own life. . . . The spiritual man, on the other hand . . . cared nothing for theology, one for whom his experience ultimately became an end in itself, without reference to the dogmatic content to be sought in it.[24]

I felt a surge of excitement. The actual dividing of spirituality and theology explained so much. No wonder Schleiermacher wanted to bring "feeling" or "intuition" back into theology. No wonder the nineteenth-century Roman Catholic theologians with six centuries of keeping theology and spirituality separate behind them were reluctant to mix the two. No wonder Nicholas of Cusa could write a great book and have it ignored for four centuries.

Bonaventure also provided another emphasis on the "coincidence of opposites" (as in Nicholas of Cusa). To him, Christ was "the first and the last, the highest and the lowest, the circumference and the center, *the Alpha and the Omega*, the cause and the caused, the Creator and the creature."[25]

During all this time of study, I had forgotten that summer almost ten years before when I had lived and breathed a single, short book. I had read it and reread it, studied, pondered, and taken notes. It helped to answer questions I had been asking about other religions since I first considered becoming a Christian. The book was Raimundo Panikkar's little volume entitled *The Trinity and the Religious Experience of Man*.[26]

Panikkar is a Christian, but he is imbued with the culture of India. Like many modern Indian Christians and increasing numbers of Westerners, Panikkar felt forced to think through the meeting ground of Hinduism and Christianity. Now, most books on spirituality that I had read did this by concentrating on meditation and contemplation. Here in the stillness, the emptiness experienced by mystics of all religions, they found a point of meeting. True, but it left me feeling that the central truth of Christianity was being slighted. If our meeting ground is solely in the emptier reaches of contemplation, what of Christ? For Christ was and is a very real person concerned with a very real world. Panikkar's thought opened the way for me to see an alternate meeting place.

Panikkar is a theologian, but not one who slights spirituality. He does not write simply, and it is too much of a simplification to say that in his book he sees Christ not only as the bridge between God and the world, but as *all bridges*, but certainly that concept is related to his thought and it is that image that stayed with me. When I had read and reread his book that summer ten years before, I had been primarily concerned about the relation between Christianity and Hinduism. Now this concept of Christ as bridge and all bridges flooded back into my mind and I saw that it was also the answer to the separation of Transcendence and Immanence, sacred and secular, church and world, for in Christ they are not separate, but together.[27]

And then, suddenly, I understood. I had come to the library to study Immanence, but it wasn't Immanence alone that interested me any more than I was interested in Transcendence alone. What made sense to me and always had was Immanence and Transcendence together, the coincidence of opposites, the Infinite and the finite, sacred and secular, church and world.

In culture as in theology, the pendulum swings; first one is emphasized and then the other. When the pendulum swings far into the world, both theologians and ordinary Christians worry about losing God. "No, God is over here!" they shout. "In the church, the Bible, the holy."

But when it swings back toward a distant Transcendent God interpreted by church and Bible and separated from the world, other people begin to turn their backs on the church. "It's just an institution," they say. "I can't understand all that theology. The Bible doesn't make sense to me."

Divorce the church from the world or the world from the church and you can have them both as far as I'm concerned. Interpret the Bible—or theology—by purely rational means unmediated by the Spirit, and they leave me cold. It was the *middle* that made sense to me, not the extremes. And in the middle was Christ—completely human and completely God. Spirit *and* flesh. God *and* world.

It is more difficult to see and to follow God in the world, in ourselves, in our neighbors, in Jesus than to pray to God in heaven. More difficult—but this is the very core of Christianity.

When I packed my bags to leave, I was at peace about my questions. There was much that I wanted to read in the future, but there was much that I *had* read and my central questions were answered. It was time to go home.[28]

18. Faith

Though earth and man were gone,
And suns and universes ceased to be,
And Thou were left alone,
Every existence would exist in Thee.

There is not room for Death,
Nor atom that his might could render void:
Thou—THOU art Being and Breath,
And what THOU art may never be destroyed.

EMILY BRONTË

To have faith in God is not to have proof. As the seventeenth-century French mathematician Blaise Pascal said, an hour after you've read the metaphysical proofs of God's existence, they vanish. God is spirit and spirit can neither be seen nor touched.[1]

Jesus, of course, *could* be seen and touched, and doubting Thomas wanted to touch as well as see the resurrected Jesus.[2] In the early church those who had seen and touched were only a generation or so in the past. Irenaeus, born one hundred years after the crucifixion, could write:

Any one who wishes to discern the truth may see in every Church in the whole world the Apostolic tradition clear and manifest. We can enumerate those who were appointed as bishops in the Churches by the Apostles and their successors to our own day. . . . Seeing that we have so many proofs, there is no need to seek among others for the truth which we can easily obtain from the Church. For the Apostles have brought fully and completely all the truth to her, lodging it with her as with a rich bank.[3]

It is pleasing to an Episcopalian to hear those words about apostolic tradition, but Irenaeus's view of the tradition was very different from ours today. As a boy, Irenaeus had known Polycarp (who lived to age eighty-six before he was martyred) and Polycarp had known the apostle John, who, of course, knew Jesus. Biblical times were that near. Not only are we farther in time from the historical Jesus, but modern biblical scholars have placed a great deal of its historical accuracy in doubt. We no longer find things anywhere near as "clear and manifest" as did Irenaeus.

I've thought about faith a good deal in the last few years and realized that it bears many different faces. Some people are cradle Christians. Faith comes to them as naturally as mother's milk. Christianity, they are taught at an early age, is what life is all about. Others, or perhaps the same people twice blessed, find God in childhood and ever after by some inborn instinct. Such was my early perception of X.

The Bible is claimed by many as a source of faith, and it is. But I wonder how many people, with no prior faith, can pick up the Bible and come to faith through its pages? As I had discovered as a young woman, reading the Bible without faith was partly interesting and partly boring but, of itself, it did not give me faith. It was only after I had realized the presence of God within me that the Bible began to come alive, and from then on, reading the Bible increased the faith I already had.

Historical accuracy or inaccuracy in the Bible has never either increased or decreased my faith. As another church father, Origen (185–254), wrote:

Occasionally the records taken in a literal sense are not true, but actually absurd and impossible, and even with the history that actually happened . . . there are other matters interwoven. . . . For our contention with regard to the whole of divine scripture is that it all has a spiritual meaning, but not all a literal meaning.[4]

It is that "spiritual meaning" as interpreted by the living God that has increased and enriched my faith.

If, then, faith is necessary before the Bible or the Christian life make sense, how do we receive faith if we have not brought it with us from childhood? "I wish I had your faith," people often say to me. The implication being that my faith is a mysterious gift. And that's true. But it is also true that it was preceded by seeking and followed by response. Respond and faith grows. Fail to respond, and it vanishes almost as quickly as metaphysical proofs. One tends to remember stories of people's sudden conversions, but in a sense all conversions are a slow, lifelong process, and many are not marked by one special turning point but by a series of ever-deepening insights.

What made me begin to think about faith was that in the darkness following my husband's death, faith faded. What kept me going was *faithfulness*. I do not use the word in the sense of "full of faith," but to connote remaining loyal even though feeling without faith. In the absence of any sense of God's presence, I had waited and watched and kept about God's business to the best of my ability.

That dark period was several years behind me now, and my life was once again both full and fulfilling. Faith was with me, but it was different. My own pain had receded, but a constant awareness of the vast and deep suffering of others remained. It was like a backdrop of darkness, and I could not dismiss it. Nor did I want to, for I knew now in a way I had not known in my younger years that wherever else in the world God may be found, God is most surely in pain and fear, in deprivation and hopelessness. Although there was faith in this knowledge, there was also a challenge to faith, for nothing challenges faith more than the question of why there is suffering and no intellectual answer seems to suffice. The best one is that God gives us freedom, and we abuse it. But that seems like a very weak argument when confronted with the suffering of multitudes of innocents during wartime or the horrors of mass deaths in natural disasters. Hearing of even one case of prolonged suffering often shakes the core of our being and makes all theological explanations seem almost blasphemous. How may we have faith in a loving God when hunger embraces innocent children, dictatorships torture people, and hopeless poverty destroys families? I didn't know, and I was often assaulted by the thought that perhaps faith was all wishful thinking and that God did not really exist.

I could not hide such thoughts in a closet of my mind and close the door on them. My faith would then be a house built on sand. But what does one do with such a question? Where does one turn to find mental confirmation of what the heart knows? For my heart *did* know. Illogical as it might seem for Love to be in charge of a suffering world that is seemingly hell-bent for destruction, my heart knew it was so. Yet, surely the mind should also enter into this matter of faith, not to prove anything, but just to say, "Yes, that makes sense." But no ready answer came to me. I would just have to watch and wait as I went on living.

I still lived in the old Victorian house, and it seemed right to be there until and unless God asked me to go elsewhere. Hospitality is neither the most dramatic nor the most sacrificial of Christian virtues, but it is one, and the house welcomed many into its ample arms. This complicated my life, and in other ways I tried to simplify, but this was a difficult task. Christianity gives us a focus that lends perspective to our complications, but it does not give an easy way out.

I found myself spending more time at the priory. To be where prayer was the norm, a way of life, and where that is the expectation was like entering another world. When I arrived, happiness would flow over me, and I would feel more at home than at home.

It was strange, I thought, when I had such a strong feeling of vocation to living in the world that the monastic life spoke to me so compellingly. As I reflected on this one day, I suddenly remembered something I had learned about Celtic Christianity: The Celtic church, unlike churches in other parts of the world, developed a monastic structure instead of a parochial one.[5] The spiritual ancestors of the people who prayed prayers as deeply involved in daily living as those recorded by Alexander Carmichael learned their faith from monks and nuns.

In my imagination I saw those ancient clusters of beehive-shaped clay and wattle or stone huts that formed their monasteries. I saw the monks and nuns who lived there and I saw simple people from the countryside coming to learn and pray at the monastery and going home again to pray as they went about their daily tasks, lit the morning fire, dressed, plowed the field, ate their supper, and laid down to rest. Was that the way it was? Perhaps not, but both the connection and the contrast were there.

Jesus withdrew from the crowds to pray, and Christianity has always kept a tradition of going on retreat to some quiet place for spiritual reflection. Not all of us can live the contemplative life all of the time even if we wanted to, but we can do so at intervals. I thought of the Buddhists of Thailand who traditionally spend a year in a monastery between ending their secular education and starting their working life. It would be good for Americans if we could do the same.

There is, of course, the other side of the coin: bringing some semblance of peace and closeness to God from the monastery out into the world. People are hungry for it. I taught a class one spring entitled, "What Is Spirituality and How Do You Find Your Own?" As it developed, it turned into a course in prayer. When the course ended, no one wanted it to be over, and ten of us decided to continue on an informal basis during the summer. "I don't know any other people," said one, "with whom I can talk about God and I need it."

I had not done any spiritual direction for several years. There had been no time. Now I wondered if I should begin again. The classic way to decide whether you should direct people is to do nothing. You do not tell friends or the clergy that you are available. You just wait and see if God sends you anyone. I decided to wait. For quite a while nothing happened, and then one hot summer day the phone rang.

A man introduced himself and said, "I read an article you wrote." Then there was hesitation and a stumbling in his voice. "Do you by any chance do spiritual direction?"

"Yes, but I haven't done any for several years."

"Then," his words came out in a rush and there was obvious relief in his voice, "you'd have room for me."

I laughed. "Yes, I would. But you don't even know me. I might not suit you at all. We'd better meet before you make up your mind."

"I've been searching and searching," he said. "I tried a couple of people, but they just weren't right. Your article was very honest, and I want someone very honest."

"Well, I *am* honest. Let's set a date, and we'll see how you feel when we meet."

And when we met, it was obvious to both of us that our working together was right. A week later a friend called on behalf of someone in another parish, and a month after that one of my students asked for direction.

Even more than in earlier years, I found direction drove me to prayer. These people trusted me to guide them into a closer relationship with God. To even write down those words is frightening. If my own relationship with God is not right, I can hurt instead of help. And so I prayed more.

The people who came to me were from very diverse backgrounds and at very different levels in their spiritual growth, yet they had at least two things in common: God was acting within them and they were responding. This was not something learned at their mother's knee, parroted from books, or caught from mass enthusiasm. This was immediate, personal, and as real as anything I knew. God is neither tangible nor visible, but you can see the effects of God's action. And I did.

Slowly I came to realize that this interior action of God, within me and within others, gave not so much an answer, but a challenge to the question: Is this all just wishful thinking? The interior action of the Holy Spirit, which led to changed lives in person after person, was much too real to call wishful thinking. If I could not dismiss suffering, neither could I dismiss God's active presence.

Once, back in my atheistic teenage years, a woman who was an old friend of my parents stopped by to visit. She had decided, she said, to join the church. Curious, I asked her why. She paused to think and then said, "There is much that is evil in the world. I want to join the good side."

I do not quote her for her theology; she might just as easily have been referring to some secular good work. I quote her because of the quiet commitment I heard in her voice, which has stayed in my mind for all these years.

Commitment. Faith grows as we respond to the grace we are given, as we commit some yet uncommitted part of ourselves to God. How was I now supposed to grow? I did not know, but I knew that God knew. I found that my visits to the priory helped as much as anything to both clarify my thoughts and encourage me. I was grateful and tried to help. "Do you need anyone to work in the garden?" I would ask. "Is there anything I could do this afternoon?" Soon I fell into a routine of writing in the mornings and working for the community in the afternoons. I felt more and more a part of their extended family.

The first time I visited the priory there was a young man there, and the prior said that the next day he would be "making a retreat."

"What do you mean?" I asked.

"Well, he won't be talking or eating with us. He'll have time alone to think and pray."

I'd thought I was already *on* retreat, but I was not, according to monastic standards. Five services a day and twelve hours of silence did not seem to be "a retreat." I felt I would like to try it. So the next time I came, I went on a day's retreat. I did some reading and a bit of writing, but mostly I just prayed. I hadn't realized that I could pray that much. I took a walk in the woods, praying as I went. I weeded the vegetable garden and prayed as I did so. I went over to the chapel and sat on a cushion and meditated. I came back to my hermitage, sat in a rocking chair, and prayed some more. The bell rang for a service and I joined the rest of the community to pray. The corporate prayer and chanting seemed all of a piece with my personal prayer, and the rhythms of the monastic life deepened within me.

The Order had a few *oblates*. I vaguely knew that an oblate was someone who was closely associated with a monastery (a priory is a small monastery) and who may or may not live there. The priory had three oblates; two lived at the priory and one did not. They had a habit, although different from the monks' habit, and they wore it to services. These matters were obvious. What else did it mean?

Oblates in this order, I discovered, all had a different agreement with the priory they were attached to. They agreed as to how often they visited and what they did when they came there. Thinking over my feelings about the priory and how I spent my time there, I realized that I had naturally fallen into a pattern of give-and-take that was similar to that of an oblate.

"I guess," I said to the prior, "that I'm about one-fifth of an oblate."

A year later I began to wonder if I could and should truly become an oblate. "Write down what you think our agreement might be," said the prior.[6] And I did. It didn't, I discovered, depart very much from what I was already doing.

The exterior actualities of being an oblate are one thing, the interior commitment is another. Related to the word *oblate* is the word *oblation*, which means offering. On the simplest level, I was offering my help to the priory. On a deeper level, I would be offering myself to God.

Commitment again. All Christians, of course, are committed to God through Christ by their baptism. What would it mean, beyond that, to offer myself to God? It meant, I realized, both a rededication and a deeper offering. The oblate's promise is to "conversion of life," conversion not once but continuous, a constant turning and returning to God, day by day, hour by hour, minute by minute. The promise, of course, did not mean that one succeeded, but it did mean that one promised to try. I did not feel ready. Another year went by before I said to the prior, "I've decided that I would like to be an oblate if you'll have me."

I was accepted as a candidate and began my year's probation. At this writing, my profession as an oblate lies two months in the future.

This tie to the monastic life is not in everyone's life and certainly was very unexpected in mine. But if I have learned anything over the years, it is that God leads one in unexpected directions.

During the last ten months, I have read quite a bit of monastic literature. One of the most useful has been an unassuming little book by a laywoman, Esther de Waal. It is called *Seeking God: The Way of St. Benedict*.[7] St. Benedict's rule is the most basic in all monasticism and one of the rules used by the monks at the priory. What Esther de Waal did in her book was to apply the rule to living in the world. This was extremely helpful to me as I was, after all, not becoming a monk or even an oblate who makes the monastery her home.

The Rule of St. Benedict is both practical and flexible, but it is also uncompromising in its spirituality. So, I discovered, was most monastic literature. Central to monasticism is "conversion of life," the very promise I was making. I began to try to practice that constant turning and returning to God that is conversion of life. Not only was I very poor at it, but I became increasingly aware of how little of my life was consciously committed to God. I was certainly more than a Sunday Christian, but many hours would go by when I didn't think of God at all, and I certainly didn't offer God each and every thought, action, and conversation. I was, I realized, a self-centered person who periodically pushed self aside to make room for God and other people.

To promise conversion of life did not mean that I would miraculously change. What it did mean was that I would be committed to try and that I would fail and turn again to God a hundred times a day.

"Even so, come, Lord Jesus."[8]

I was professed an oblate of the Order of The Holy Cross at Holy Savior Priory in Pineville, South Carolina, on April 23, 1988.

Notes

Epigraph, page vii: John W. Harvey, Preface to *The Idea of the Holy*, by Rudolf Otto, trans., John W. Harvey, (London: Oxford University Press, 1923), p. xi. (This preface does not appear in later editions.)

CHAPTER 1: WITHIN AND BEYOND

Epigraph: St. Bernard of Clairvaux, *Epistle 106*.

1. The house was in the South County of Rhode Island. It fact, there is no county called "South," but the name is used locally—and fondly—to refer to the southern part of the state that is near the ocean.
2. St. Martin's Episcopal Church in Providence, Rhode Island.
3. Westover School in Middlebury, Connecticut.
4. The Rhode Island School of Design (RISD) in Providence, Rhode Island.

CHAPTER 2: THE KINGDOM OF GOD

1. Darien, Connecticut.
2. Luke 17:21, King James Version.
3. Saint Luke's Church, Darien, Connecticut.

CHAPTER 3: SACRAMENT

Epigraph: Evelyn Underhill, *Man and the Supernatural* (London: Methuen, 1927), pp. 181–82.

1. May be found, among other places, in the catechism in *The Book of Common Prayer* (New York, Seabury, 1979), p. 857.
2. Ibid., p. 413.
3. Acts 8:14–17; 19:1–7.
4. Acts 2:1–3.
5. Luke 22:19; 1 Cor. 11:24–25.
6. *The New York Times*, May 9, 1959.
7. Charles Williams, *All Hallow's Eve* (Grand Rapids, MI: Eerdmans, 1981).

CHAPTER 4: A GUIDE

Epigraph: Tilden Edwards, *Spiritual Friend: Reclaiming the Gift of Spiritual Direction* (New York: Paulist, 1980), p. 105.

1. General Theological Seminary, New York, New York.
2. Luke 1:34.

CHAPTER 5: INTERLUDE IN INDIA

Epigraph: Ramakrishna, *The Sayings of Sri Ramakrishna* (New York: Vedanta Society, 1903).

1. Darien, Connecticut, and Mercara (now called Madikeri), Karnataka, India.
2. Hallam Tennyson, *India's Walking Saint: The Story of Vinoba Bhave* (New York, Doubleday, 1955).
3. Ibid., p. 118.
4. Ibid., p. 118–19.
5. Christopher Isherwood, *Ramakrishna and His Disciples* (New York: Simon and Schuster, 1959, 1965).

CHAPTER 6: GOD AND THE BIBLE

Epigraph: Søren Kierkegaard, *For Self Examination* (Copenhagen, 1851). I am unable to locate the translation quoted. In Walter Lowrie's translation (Princeton, NJ: Princeton University Press, 1944), it reads: "In reading God's Word thou must continually say to thyself, 'It is to me this is addressed, it is about me it speaks'" (p. 68).

1. J. B. Phillips, *The Young Church in Action* (New York: Macmillan, 1958).
2. Acts 1:3–10.
3. Acts 2.
4. Matthew 27:46; Mark 15:34, King James Version.
5. Matthew 13:33; Luke 13:20–21.
6. Luke 15:8.
7. Matthew 13:31–32; Mark 4:30–32; Luke 13:18–19.
8. Matthew 13:9; Mark 4:23; Luke 8:8.
9. Matthew 13:45–46 (my own paraphrase).
10. Matthew 13:31–32; Mark 4:30–32; Luke 13:18–19 (my own paraphrase).

CHAPTER 7: SAINTS WITH A SMALL S

Epigraph: John Macquarrie, *Principles of Christian Theology* (New York: Scribner, 1966), p. 187.

1. John 3:8, King James Version.
2. J. N. D. Kelly, *Early Christian Creeds*, 2d ed., (New York: David McKay, 1960), p. 391.

CHAPTER 8: THE LARGER COMPANY

1. St. Christopher has not been completely cast out by the Catholic church, but he is no longer on the universal calendar. His story was preserved in *The Golden Legend* and is retold in many places.
2. There are many biographies of St. Teresa. An excellent modern one is Stephen Clissold, *St. Teresa of Avila* (New York: Seabury, 1982).
3. Teresa of Avila, *Life* (chapter 8, section 2). My friend Francis Tiso once translated this quotation for me from the original Spanish in St. Teresa's autobiography. I find his words more lyrical than available published translations in English although the meaning is obviously the same.

4. Ibid., section 7.
5. A good biography of John Vianney: Michel de Saint Pierre, *The Remarkable Curé of Ars*, trans. M. Angeline Bouchard (New York: Doubleday, 1963).
6. Ida Goerres, *The Hidden Face: The Life of Thérèse of Lisieux*, trans. Richard and Clara Winston (New York: Pantheon, 1959).
7. John McNeill, *The Celtic Churches* (Chicago: University of Chicago Press, 1974), p. 95.
8. Peers, *The Life of Teresa of Jesus*, p. 191.
9. There are a number of biographies of Mary Slessor. An excellent modern one is James Buchan, *The Expendable Mary Slessor* (New York: Seabury, 1981).
10. Buchan, *The Expendable Mary Slessor*, p. 195.
11. Ibid., p. 99.
12. John Woolman, *The Journal of John Woolman*. See Douglas Steere, ed., *Quaker Spirituality: Selected Writings* (New York: Paulist, 1984).
13. Desmond Doig, *Mother Teresa: Her People and Her Work* (New York: Harper & Row, 1976).
14. Dag Hammarskjöld, *Markings* (New York: Knopf, 1964).

CHAPTER 9: GOD IN EVERYDAY LIFE

Epigraph: Gershom G. Scholem, *Jewish Mysticism* (Princeton, NJ: Princeton University Press, 1973), p. 216.

1. Actually I read three books on the laity. The most useful was Charles Neill and Hans-Ruedi Weber, eds., *The Layman in Christian History* (Philadelphia: Westminster, 1963). The others were Alden D. Kelley, *The People of God: A Study in the Doctrine of the Laity* (Greenwich, CT: Seabury, 1962) and Howard Grimes, *The Rebirth of the Laity* (Nashville, TN: Abingdon, 1962).
2. Martin Buber, *Tales of the Hasidim: Early Masters* (New York: Schocken, 1946); *Tales of the Hasidim: Later Masters* (New York: Schocken, 1948); *The Origin and Meaning of Hasidim* (New York: Horizon Press, 1960; Harper & Row, 1966).
3. The first women received degrees from General Theological Seminary, the Episcopal seminary in New York City, in 1974.
4. Union Theological Seminary in New York City.
5. The version I read at the time came from the 1928 edition of *The Book of Common Prayer*. The version I quote, from the 1979 edition, has been slightly changed.
6. Pierre Teilhard de Chardin, *The Divine Milieu* (New York: Harper & Row, 1960), pp. 82–83.
7. Thomas Kelly, *Testament of Devotion* (New York: Harper, 1941), p. 29.
8. Michel Quoist, *Prayers* trans. Agnes Forsyth and Anne Marie de Commaille (New York: Sheed and Ward, 1963), p. 11.
9. Ibid., p. 29.

CHAPTER 10: BIBLICAL MEDITATION

Epigraph: Suzanne de Dietrich, *God's Word in Today's World* (Valley Forge, PA: Judson, 1967), p. 30.

1. Bede Frost, *The Art of Mental Prayer* (London: SPCK, 1931, 1954).
2. Mark 10:46–52.

CHAPTER 11: SPIRITUAL DIRECTION

Epigraph: St. Isaac the Syrian, quoted in E. Kadloubovsky and G. E. H. Palmer, *Early Fathers from the Philokalia* (London: Faber and Faber, 1964), p. 162.

1. C. S. Lewis, *The Four Loves* (New York: Harcourt, Brace and World, 1960), pp. 87–127.

CHAPTER 12: HOW TO MEDITATE WITHOUT LEAVING THE WORLD

Epigraph: *Midrash*, Exodus Rabbath 2:9.

1. Avery Brooke, *How to Meditate Without Leaving the World* (Noroton, CT: Vineyard, 1975). I am currently working on a revised edition.
2. My friends in India sent me the following books: M. K. Gandhi, *An Autobiography or the Story of My Experiments with Truth* (Ahmedabad: Navajivan Publishing House, 1927); M. K. Gandhi, *Non-Violence in Peace and War* (Ahmedabad: Navajivan Publishing House, 1949); Mahadev Desai, *The Gita According to Gandhi* (Ahmedabad: Navajivan Publishing House, 1946); C. Rajagopalachari, *Ramayana* (Bombay: Bharatiya Vidya Bharan, 1958); *The Chicago Addresses*, Swami Vivekananda (Calcutta: Udbodhan Office; the original addresses were made at the World's Parliament of Religions in Chicago in 1893).
3. Verses 2 and 3 of a poem written by an anonymous member of the Beguines, a religious sisterhood in the Netherlands in the twelfth century. The poem is from a thirteenth-century collection entitled *Mengeldichten* and here quoted from Jean Leclercq, Francois Vandenbroucke, and Louis Bouyer, *The Spirituality of the Middle Ages* (New York: Seabury, 1963), pp. 362–363.

CHAPTER 13: SPIRITUAL AND PSYCHOLOGICAL GROWTH

Epigraph: *Meister Eckhart*, quoted in Raymond Bernard Blakney, *Meister Eckhart: A Modern Translation* (New York: Harper, 1941).

1. Union Theological Seminary in New York City.
2. I started with Sigmund Freud, *A General Introduction to Psychoanalysis* (New York: Washington Square Press, 1952–1958) and *New Introductory Lectures on Psychoanalysis*, trans. James Strachey, (New York: Norton, 1964).
3. Carl Jung, *Analytical Psychology: Its Theory and Practice* (New York: Random House, 1970).
4. I read most of Erik Erikson's work, but found the following particularly helpful: *Identity and the Life Cycle*, Psychological Issues, Vol. 1, no. 1, (New York: International Universities Press, 1959); *Childhood and Society* (New York: Norton, 1950, 1963); *Insight and Responsibility* (New York: Norton, 1964). Years later I was happy to encourage the publication of an excellent book by J. Eugene Wright, Jr., *Erikson: Identity and Religion* (New York: Seabury, 1982).
5. Harry Stack Sullivan, *Conceptions of Modern Psychiatry* (New York: Norton, 1933); *Personal Psychopathology* (New York: Norton, 1972); *The Interpersonal Theory of Psychiatry* (New York: Norton, 1953); *The Psychiatric Interview* (New York: Norton, 1954); *Clinical Studies in Psychiatry* (New York: Norton, 1956).

The reader may also be interested in the excellent biography of Sullivan by Helen Swick Perry, *Psychiatrist of America: The Life of Harry Stack Sullivan* (Cambridge, MA, and London: Harvard University Press, Belknap Press, 1982).

6. Michel Quoist, *Prayers*, trans. Agnes Forsyth and Anne Marie de Commaille (New York: Sheed and Ward, 1963).

Chapter 14: Knowledge and Action

Epigraph: B. D. Napier, *A Quintet from Genesis* (Philadelphia: United Church Press, 1967), p. 17.

1. Paul Tillich, *Systematic Theology*, 3 vols. (Chicago: University of Chicago Press, 1951, 1957, 1963).
2. Strangely, considering the impact it had, the book of essays has long since vanished from my shelves and its title from my memory.
3. Matthew 16:15–16.
4. A good book on the creeds is J. N. D. Kelly's *Early Christian Doctrines* (New York: Harper & Row, 1958, 1960).
5. Matthew 8:21–22; Luke 9:59–60 (my own paraphrase).
6. Matthew 19:21 (my own paraphrase).
7. Walter Lowrie, *Kierkegaard* (New York: Harper & Row, 1962).
8. Dietrich Bonhoeffer, *Letters and Papers from Prison* (New York: Macmillan, 1962); *The Cost of Discipleship* (New York: Macmillan, 1963).
9. Person to Person, St. Luke's Church, Darien, Connecticut.
10. Thomas Kelly, *A Testament of Devotion* (New York: Harper, 1941), p. 109.
11. Gerard Manley Hopkin's "Pied Beauty" is available in many collections including Helen Gardner's *Book of Religious Verse* (New York: Oxford University Press, 1972), p. 289.
12. Woodstock Seminary, affiliated with Union Theological Seminary in New York City.

Chapter 15: Seeking an Immanent Spirituality

Epigraph: Clyde A. Holbrook, "The Ambiguities of Transcendence," *The Christian Century* 92, no. 483 (December 24, 1975): 1180–83.

1. Vineyard Books, Noroton, Connecticut.
2. John Macquarrie, *Paths in Spirituality* (New York: Harper & Row, 1972), p. 122.
3. Alexander Carmichael, ed. and trans., *Carmina Gadelica: Hymns and Incantations, vol. I* (Edinburgh: Oliver and Boyd, 1900). In 1977 I selected prayers from volume 1 that were published by Vineyard Books under the title *Celtic Invocations*. In 1981 I selected prayers from volume 3, and these were published by Seabury under the title *Celtic Prayers*.
4. Avery Brooke, ed., *Celtic Prayers* (New York: Seabury, 1981), p. 17.
5. W. C. Mackenzie, *History of the Outer Hebrides* (Edinburgh: James Thin, Mercat Press, 1974).
6. Alice Benjamin and Harriett Corrigan, *Cooking with Conscience* (Noroton, CT: Vineyard, 1975).

7. The Seabury Press, New York City, now a part of Harper & Row, San Francisco.
8. Avery Brooke et al., *The Vineyard Bible* (New York: Seabury, 1980).

CHAPTER 16: DARKNESS AND LIGHT

Epigraphs: Psalm 139:10–11 quoted from *The Book of Common Prayer* (New York: Seabury, 1979), p. 794. John 8:12 (my own paraphrase).

1. The Fund for Peace in New York City.
2. *First Steps to Peace* (New York: The Fund for Peace, 1985 and subsequent revisions).
3. Holy Savior Priory, a monastery of the Order of the Holy Cross in Pineville, South Carolina.

CHAPTER 17: WITH ALL YOUR MIND

Epigraph: Raimundo Panikkar, *The Trinity and the Religious Experience of Man* (New York: Orbis, 1973), p. 74.

1. Louis Bouyer, *Dictionary of Theology*, trans. Charles Underhill Quinn, (New York: Desclee, 1963), p. 225.
2. St. Deiniol's Library, Hawarden, Wales.
3. Benedict de Spinoza (1632–1677). For the most useful American edition see Edwin Curley's translation, *The Collected Works of Spinoza* (Princeton, NJ: Princeton University Press, 1985).
4. Meister Eckhart (1260–1327). The most easily available American editions are two in the *Classics of Western Spirituality* series: *Meister Eckhart: Teacher and Preacher*, Edmund Colledge, O.S.A. and Bernard McGinn, Frank Tobin and Elvira Borgstadt, eds. (New York: Paulist, 1986) and *Meister Eckhart: The Essential Sermons, Commentaries, Treatises, and Defense*, Edmund Colledge, O.S.A. and Bernard McGinn, eds. (New York: Paulist, 1981). I also like Raymond Bernard Blakney's *Meister Eckhart: A Modern Translation* (New York: Harper, 1941).
5. Nicholas of Cusa (Nicolaus Cusanus; ca. 1400–1464). His major work, *Of Learned Ignorance*, is available in a translation by Germain Heron (New Haven, CT: Yale University Press, 1954).
6. The Modernists were a group of Roman Catholic scholars in a variety of fields. Leading figures in the group were George Tyrrell, Alfred Loisy, and F. von Hügel. Maurice Blondel is often grouped with the Modernists, but his work was not condemned. The controversy is well described in Gabriel Daly, *Transcendence and Immanence: A Study in Catholic Modernism and Integralism* (Oxford: Clarendon, 1980). A more informal account is conveyed in Michael de la Bedoyere's *The Life of Baron von Hügel* (New York: Scribner, 1951).
7. Teilhard de Chardin (1881–1955). His two major works are *The Phenomenon of Man* (New York: Harper & Row, 1959) and *The Divine Milieu* (New York: Harper & Row, 1960).
8. These remarks about Spinoza appear in Thomas McFarland's *Coleridge and the Pantheist Tradition* (Oxford: Clarendon, 1919), pp.72–74. Samuel Taylor

Coleridge, known to most of us as a poet, was also a philosopher. He helped bring Spinoza back into esteem.

9. *The Collected Works of Spinoza,* ed. and trans. Edwin Curley, (Princeton, NJ: Princeton University Press, 1985), vol. 1, p. 401.

10. Ibid., p. 4.

11. Paul Tillich, *Perspective on Nineteenth and Twentieth Century Protestant Theology* (New York: Harper & Row, 1967), pp. 74, 94–95.

12. Ibid., pp. 73–74. Also Thomas McFarland, *Coleridge and the Pantheist Tradition* (London: Oxford: Clarendon, 1969), pp. 76–87.

13. Friedrich Schleiermacher (1768–1834), *Religion, Speeches to Its Cultured Despisers* and *The Christian Faith,* ed. H. R. Mackintosh and J. S. Steward (New York: Harper & Row, 1963).

14. Tillich, *Perspectives,* p. 96.

15. Gabriel Daly, *Transcendence and Immanence: A Study in Catholic Modernism and Integralism* (New York: Oxford: Clarendon 1980), p. 9.

16. Ibid., pp. 10–21.

17. Ibid., p. 19.

18. Ibid., p. 25.

19. Michael de la Bedoyere, *The Life of Baron von Hügel* (New York: Scribner, 1951). Although I make no direct quotes, this book helped me tremendously in understanding the Modernist controversy.

20. Nicholas Cusanus, *Of Learned Ignorance,* trans. Germain Heron, (New Haven, CT: Yale University Press, 1954). (Nicholas Cusanus is more often entitled Nicholas of Cusa).

21. Ibid, p. 83.

22. Tillich, *Perspectives,* p. 77.

23. Ewert Cousins, ed. *Introduction to Bonaventure* (New York: Paulist, 1978), pp. 1–2. For a more detailed treatment see Ewert Cousins, *Bonaventure and the Coincidence of Opposites* (Chicago: Franciscan Herald Press, 1978) and *Bonaventure, the Coincidence of Opposites and Nicholas of Cusa* in *Studies Honoring Ignatius Charles Brady, Friar Minor,* ed. Romano Stephen Almagno, O.F.M., and Conrad L. Harkins (St. Bonaventure, NY: Franciscan Institute, 1976), pp. 177–197.

24. Louis Bouyer, Jean Leclercq, and Francois Vandenbroucke, *The Spirituality of the Middle Ages* (New York: Seabury, 1963), pp. 371–372

25. Ewert Cousins, ed., *Introduction to Bonaventure* (New York: Paulist, 1978), pp. 108–109.

26. Raimundo Panikkar, *The Trinity and the Religious Experience of Man* (New York: Orbis, 1973).

27. Ibid. Although Panikkar writes of the Trinity in this book, he ends by turning to *theandrism,* which he says "is the classical and traditional term for that intimate and complete unity which is realized paradigmatically in Christ between the divine and the human and which is the goal towards which everything here below tends" (p. 71).

28. Although I read a great deal on this trip to St. Deiniol's, much of my reading was done over many years and just came to fruition on this and a subsequent trip to Wales. I have telescoped time to enable me to put my thoughts in story form.

Two areas of thought I did not discuss should at least be mentioned. One is Anglican theology. Anglican writers, in general, tend to be more comfortable with Immanence than are members of other denominations. This may be primarily because the Incarnation has always been important to Anglicans, but we are probably also influenced by our Celtic inheritance. Anglicans tend to give their primary allegiance to worship and our theology is, therefore, closer to spirituality. Faced as I was with a vast amount of material, it was easiest to see and write about Immanence where the issues were more clearly drawn by conflict. Of particular interest to Anglicans is Archbishop William Temple's *Nature, Man and God* (London: Macmillan, 1960) and any of the work of A. M. Allchin, particularly *The World Is a Wedding* (New York: Oxford, 1978).

Another important issue I left undiscussed for reasons of simplification is Karl Barth's emphasis on God transcendent. For those interested, I recommend two books by John Baillie, *The Sense of the Presence of God* (New York: Scribner, 1962) and *Our Knowledge of God* (New York: Scribner, 1959).

CHAPTER 18: FAITH

Epigraph: Emily Brontë, "No Coward Soul Is Mine," verses 5–6, available in many collections including Oscar Williams, *The Mentor Book of Major British Poets* (New York: New American Library, 1963), p. 292.

1. Blaise Pascal, *Pensées*, trans. A. J. Kraitsheimer (Harmondsworth, England, and Baltimore, MD: Penguin Books, 1966), #190, p. 86. (The wording is my paraphrase.)
2. John 20:24–29.
3. Irenaeus, *Against Heresies*, Book 3 of *The Faith in Scripture and Tradition* as quoted in Hugh T. Kerr, *Readings in Christian Thought* (Nashville, TN: Abingdon, 1966), p. 33.
4. Cyril C. Richardson et al., *Early Christian Fathers* (Philadelphia: Westminster, 1953), vol. 1, p. 347.
5. Among the most useful references are John T. McNeill, *The Celtic Churches: A History, a.d. 200–1200* (Chicago: University of Chicago Press, 1974) and Kathleen Hughes and Ann Hamlin, *Celtic Monasticism: The Modern Traveler to the Early Irish Church* (New York: Seabury, 1981).
6. All oblates of the Order of the Holy Cross work out individual agreements with the prior of the monastery to which they are attached. The agreements specify what the oblate will do for the monastery and the monastery for the oblate. The agreement is in addition to the oblate's promise.
7. Esther de Waal, *Seeking God: The Way of St. Benedict* (Collegeville, MN: Liturgical Press, 1984).
8. Rev. 22:20. This is the next to last line in the Bible in the King James Version.

Index